ABA Career Series

Nonlegal Careers for Lawyers

5th edition

Gary A. Munneke
William D. Henslee
Ellen Wayne

ABA **LawPracticeManagementSection**
MARKETING · MANAGEMENT · TECHNOLOGY · FINANCE

American Bar Association
Law Student Division

Commitment to Quality: The Law Practice Management Section is committed to quality in our publications. Our authors are experienced practitioners in their fields. Prior to publication, the contents of all our books are rigorously reviewed by experts to ensure the highest quality product and presentation. Because we are committed to serving our readers' needs, we welcome your feedback on how we can improve future editions of this book.

Cover design by Gail Patejunas.

Library of Congress Cataloging-in-Publication Data

Munneke, Gary A.
   Nonlegal careers for lawyers / by Gary A. Munneke, William D. Henslee, Ellen S. Wayne.—5th ed.
       p. cm.
   Includes bibliographical references and index.
   ISBN 1-59031-675-4 (alk. paper)
   1. Lawyers–United States. 2. Law–Vocational guidance–United States.
I. Henslee, William D. II. Wayne, Ellen S. III. American Bar Association. IV. Title.

   KF297.M862 2006
   340.023'73–dc22   2006011320

1 2 3 4 5 6 7 11   11 09 08 07 06

Contents

PART III
Resources   **153**

Preface

The American Bar Association's Career Series is designed to give students and beginning lawyers practical information on choosing and following career paths in the practice of law. Books in the series offer realistic, firsthand accounts of practicing law in specific substantive areas, and guidance on setting and reaching career goals.

The Career Series is the joint effort of the Law Practice Management Section and the Law Student Division of the American Bar Association. Originally created during the ABA's 1982 Annual Meeting by the Section of Economics of Law Practice (now the Section of Law Practice Management), the Law Student Division, and the Standing Committee on Professional Utilization and Career Development, the Career Series has produced timely practical career-oriented books for law students for over two decades.

The goal of the Career Series is to help lawyers secure satisfying jobs in their chosen areas of practice. To this end, the authors present this publication to complement the Career Series library of titles.

Gary A. Munneke
Professor of Law
Pace University
School of Law

Ellen Wayne
Dean of Career Services
Columbia University
School of Law

William D. Henslee
Associate Professor of Law
Florida A&M University
School of Law

Acknowledgments

The first edition of *Nonlegal Careers for Lawyers* was written by Frances Utley in 1980, and, over the years, many people have worked to produce the next four editions of the book and other titles in the ABA Career Series. Among the editors whose insights have guided the authors are Professor Joan Bullock, Theodore Orenstein, Monica Bay, and Percy Luney. Numerous American Bar Association staff members have supported the work of the authors and editors. These professionals have included Beverly Loder, Patricia Brennan, Neal Cox, Tim Johnson, Sherry Gouwens, Kathy Wiley, Jane Johnston, and Paula Tsurutani. In addition, various officers and leaders of the Law Student Division, as well as Professor Munneke's students at Pace Law School, have reviewed and commented on the early drafts of this book. The authors thank all of these individuals for their contributions, because without them it would be impossible to keep the information in this book current and relevant.

About the Authors

Gary A. Munneke is a professor of law at Pace University School of Law, in White Plains, New York, where he teaches courses in professional responsibility, torts, and law practice management. Prior to his tenure at Pace, he was a professor at Widener University School of Law and assistant dean at the University of Texas School of Law. At the University of Texas, he was one of the first lawyers in the United States with exclusive responsibility for career services, and the career services model he created at the University of Texas in the 1970s has since been adopted by nearly every American law school.

Professor Munneke is active as a leader of the American Bar Association, having been elected to the ABA Board of Governors in 2006, after serving as a member of the ABA House of Delegates, as Chair of the Law Practice Management Section, as Chair of the Section's Publishing Board, and as a member of the ABA Standing Committee on Publishing Oversight. He has also served as President of the National Association for Law Placement and participated in a number of other committees for the ABA and other professional associations.

Professor Munneke is the author of numerous books and articles about current issues on the legal profession, the practice of law and legal career issues, including *Barron's How to Succeed in Law School, Barron's Guide to Law Schools, The Legal Career Guide: From Law Student to Lawyer, Careers in Law, Opportunities in Law*

Careers, Careers in Law, Seize the Future: Forecasting and Influencing the Future of the Legal Profession, Materials and Cases on Law Practice Management, Law Practice Management in a Nutshell, and *The Essential Formbook: Comprehensive Management Tools for Lawyers.* Professor Munneke is a frequent speaker at seminars and conferences on topics related to his teaching and writing.

A 1973 graduate of the University of Texas School of Law, Professor Munneke is a member of the Texas and Pennsylvania bars, the New York State Bar Association, and the Association of the Bar of the City of New York. He is the New York Co-Chair of the Fellows of the American Bar Foundation, and a Fellow of the College of Law Practice Management.

William D. Henslee is an associate professor of law at Florida A&M College of Law, in Orlando, Florida. He teaches real property, copyright law, entertainment law, sports law, travel law, law and the media, and a seminar on special problems in music law. Before becoming a member of the FAMU faculty, he taught for twelve years at Pepperdine University School of Law. Professor Henslee serves as Chair of the ABA Career Series Steering Committee and editor of the Career Series. He has served as the Chair of the ABA Law Student Division's Competitions Committee and has served on the National Appellate Advocacy Competition Subcommittee and the Negotiation Competition Subcommittee. He is a member of the ABA Law Practice Management Section Publishing Board and has served on the Section's Council. Professor Henslee served as the Chair of the ABA Standing Committee on Professional Utilization and Career Development. He is a former Chair of the ABA Law Student Division. Before his term as Chair, he served as the ninth circuit governor.

Professor Henslee is the author of the Career Series books *Entertainment Law Careers* (1998) and *Careers in Entertainment Law* (1990), and the Law Student Division publication *How to Survive the First Year of Law School* (1996, 1986). In addition, he has served as editor for all of the books in the Career Series: *Careers in Labor Law,* by Ellen Wayne; *Careers in Natural Resources and Environmental Law,* by Percy R. Luney Jr.; *Careers in Sports Law,* by Kenneth L. Shropshire; *Careers in Civil Litigation,* by Monica Bay; and *The Legal Career Guide: From Law Student to Lawyer,* by Gary A. Munneke. He is the coauthor of the textbooks *Travel Law,* by Robert M. Jarvis, John R. Goodwin, and William D. Henslee (Carolina Academic Press, 1998), *Entertainment Law,* with Sherri Burr (West, 2004), and *Theater Law,* with Robert Jarvis, et al. (Carolina Academic Press, 2004).

Professor Henslee has owned a music publishing company since 1986. Over the past few years, he has produced the films *Joshua Tree, Bishop,* and *The Karaoke King.* He has been a certified contract advisor for the NFL since 1994.

Professor Henslee earned a master of fine arts degree from the University of California, Los Angeles, Graduate School of Film and Television in 1996. He is a 1984 graduate of Pepperdine University School of Law. He is a member of the California, New Mexico, and Pennsylvania bars. He received his bachelor's degree from the University of Hawaii in 1977.

Ellen Wayne is the dean of career services at Columbia University School of Law in New York, NY. She administers an office that is charged with the career counseling of more than 1,300 J.D. students and 200 international L.L.M students and the management of some of the largest recruitment programs in the country. In her role as career counselor, she regularly assists students and graduates of the law school with their career choices.

Dean Wayne is the author of numerous articles, including a career column written for the *New York Law Journal* and reprinted by the *National Law Journal* and other legal periodicals and online publications. She has also written the Career Series book *Careers in Labor Law,* published by the American Bar Association.

Dean Wayne has also spoken about trends in the legal profession, career counseling and resource information, professionalism and ethics, the MacCrate Report (published by the American Bar Association), and other topics relevant to the legal profession at many professional association meetings, including American Bar Association annual meeting programs for the Business Law Section, the Section on Legal Education, and, most often, for the Law Practice Management Section.

Dean Wayne is active in many legal associations, including having served as the Chair of the Student Services Section of the Association of American Law Schools; as an Officer of the National

Association for Law Placement; as a member of the Association of the Bar of the City of New York's Recruitment and Retention Committee; the New York State Bar Committee on Legal Education and Admission to the Bar; and as Vice Chair of the Education Board of the American Bar Association's Law Practice Management Section; and as Co-Chair of the Committee on Professional Competence and Liability for the General Practice Section.

Dean Wayne has a M.Ed. in counseling and administration from Northeastern University.

Pursuing a Nonlegal Career

Introduction

1

The phrase "Nonlegal Careers for Lawyers" may seem perplexing to some. What do lawyers do if not practice law? Why would a person invest in three or four years of law school to do something she could do without obtaining a legal education? How can a career be legal and nonlegal at the same time?

This book provides some answers to these questions. The fact that legally trained individuals work both inside and outside the practice of law is indisputable. According to American Bar Foundation statistics, slightly more than 60 percent of the one million lawyers in the United States engage in the private practice of law (i.e., delivering legal services to clients for profit). Of those in the remaining 40 percent, many work in legal positions in corporate legal and government legal departments and other institutional forms of law practice.

At the same time, a great many of the 40 percent who are not engaged in private practice work for organizations, or for themselves, in enterprises where licensure or even law school graduation is not a prerequisite. A recurring theme of this book is that legal training and the application of legal skills can benefit lawyers who pursue these positions. In some cases, a law degree may help someone to succeed in a field outside the practice of law. In other cases, legal experience may afford a law graduate a decided advantage over those who have not been to law school. The old adage "a lawyer can learn about business, but an MBA will never learn the law" may not sit well with business school supporters, but it reflects a basic truth about the flexibility of a law degree.

Throughout this book the authors have created a series of descriptive sketches (appearing as shaded sidebars) of law school graduates who have pursued nonlegal careers. Although the names have been changed, most of the sketches are based on real people; a few of the stories are composites of several individuals. Collectively, these snapshots provide real-life examples of people who have done what you are thinking about doing. The fact that you are looking at this book is an indication that you or someone you care about is thinking about a nonlegal career. We hope that seeing these examples will help you to visualize the opportunities open to you.

▼▼▼▼▼

George hated getting up each morning and going to work. His job in a midsized law firm was no longer exciting to him; in fact, he felt no personal satisfaction in the work he did. George saw no future in the practice of law, so he rebelled by seeking a new career. What set George apart from other lawyers was that he had been a partner with the same prominent law firm for the past twenty-five years.

▼▼▼▼▼

After graduating from law school, Donna spent months interviewing for a job without success. She finally found a sole practitioner who needed an associate. Donna got paid a percentage of the fees she billed, a livelihood that fell far short of her law school expectations, and she sometimes felt that her work could have been done by an average third-grader. So Donna decided to look for a career outside the law in a field that excited and challenged her in a way that her work as a lawyer did not.

▼▼▼▼▼

Natalie started law school to fulfill a lifelong dream. It was not long before she began to doubt her career choice. Law school was not as exciting as she had expected; on the contrary, she found it aggravating and boring. Still, she managed to perform adequately and followed her classmates in pursuit of high-paying summer associate positions. When talking to her law school career counselor, however, all her doubts about law came to a head. In midstream, she stopped interviewing law firms and began her search for a nonlegal job.

▼▼▼▼▼

Xavier had worked his way up the corporate ladder before coming to law school, and he kept his job throughout his legal education. Xavier had always wanted to be a lawyer, but the finances were just not there when he graduated from college as a young, unemployed parent. Xavier enjoyed law but soon recognized that he would take a substantial cut in pay, status, and independence by becoming an entry-level lawyer. So Xavier, like many others, finished his law degree and continued working in his old job.

These cases may not seem like typical law students and lawyers, but they are not unusual. Although many lawyers find satisfaction in the challenge of their work, many others are frustrated and unhappy. Some are turning away from traditional legal careers; many other lawyers suffer in silence.

Many law school graduates experience a disquieting feeling that the traditional practice of law was not the career choice they had envisioned when they started their law school training. Others recognize that they made a mistake after a few years in practice. Still others discover their legal and nonlegal interests metamorphosing and melding into new and exciting enterprises. Very often these people have been reluctant to move away from traditional practice, assuming that a nonlegal career would mean opting for a second-rate choice.

These feelings may be magnified by family and friends, who are unfamiliar with the many alternatives available to lawyers today. They may have visions of you unemployed or stuck in a minimum-wage job and issue dire warnings. Yet there are lawyer corporation presidents, lawyer doctors, lawyer hockey players, lawyer sportscasters, and lawyer actors and actresses, to name but a few.

The story of Alan Levin is typical of the many lawyers whose experience in a nonlegal career has been a good one. As a student at the Delaware Law School (now Widener University School of Law), Alan served as chair of the ABA Law Student Division in 1979–1980. After graduation, he began what could have been a traditional career in the practice of law. When his father, Harry Levin, became ill, however, Alan was needed to assist with the family business, Happy Harry's, a small chain of drug stores in Delaware. Alan continued to work in the business, which he took over upon his father's death. In the ensuing years, he built Happy Harry's into a retail powerhouse in the mid-Atlantic region. Although he never returned to the practice of law, his legal training undoubtedly contributed to his success in the business world.

You may not become a corporate president like Alan Levin, a major-league baseball manager like Tony La Russa, or a best-selling author like John Grisham, but you can do something with your law degree other than practice law. This book is about nonlegal careers that are realistically attainable by those whose legal training provides a leg up in the business world. The positions presented are either entry-level or early-advancement points that afford opportunities to attain even higher positions later. Not one is presented as a second choice or dead end in terms of its potential.

These nonlegal careers have a special appeal to people who are trained in the law and have other areas of experience. If you are one of these people, your legal training expands your career potential dramatically because you now offer special skills that have dozens of applications in your chosen field.

Law school broadens career potential for someone who specializes in another field as well as for the new lawyer who simply knows that traditional law practice is not for him or her. A summer job in a law firm might lead to the conclusion that you do not want to do this for the rest of your life, but the thought of wasting your legal education panics you. Rather than think of it as wasted time and money, you need to envision how a law degree can help you in any career you choose.

If you are just beginning to think about a career outside of the traditional practice of law, though, you probably feel uncertain as to just where to start. This uncertainty is understandable. The number of choices open to you is virtually limitless. In fact, judging from the experience of those who have chosen this career path before you, the choice is limited only by your imagination and the career goals you set for yourself.

To help you focus the direction of your career planning and attain your first position, this book suggests broad areas of nonlegal work in which lawyers are currently employed. As you read, keep asking yourself, Would this type of work interest me? Would I be good at this type of work? If I started at this point, what might my future plans and development include?

Once you have selected areas that appear promising based on your gut reaction, you can begin to include more information and depth in your search. Until you reach a final decision, however, keep an open mind. The range of nonlegal careers for lawyers is developing rapidly. New possibilities may develop even as you explore the opportunities currently open to you.

This book is organized into three parts:

- ◆ The first part examines nonlegal careers generally, and discusses a model for assessing nonlegal career opportunities and the steps to follow for seeking a nonlegal position.
- ◆ The second part describes a number of nonlegal careers that lawyers have chosen; these descriptions are not meant to be exhaustive, but they do cover the most common nonlegal-career paths for lawyers.
- ◆ The third part includes resources for nonlegal careers, including books, articles, Web sites, lists, and other useful information. One of the most daunting aspects to such a career search is the sheer volume of information involved, so this section is intended to jump-start your research efforts.

Even if you decide not to pursue a career outside the law, the process of introspection can be helpful in finding a comfort level for whatever decision you make. If you decide to practice law while harboring lingering doubts about your choice, you may find career satisfaction elusive. If you make a choice after considering all the options, however, you are more likely to find happiness with your selection.

As a final note, you do not have to read this book from cover to cover. Some of the chapters may not apply to you, and others may cover concepts you already understand. Use those sections that help you and skip the ones that do not. Remember that this book is a tool to help you, not a class or work assignment.

If you decide on a nonlegal career, you will join a club with many members, some famous, some obscure, some rich, some not so rich, some happy, and some . . . well, some people just cannot find happiness. However you end up, you will certainly not be alone.

The Legal Profession | **2**

Lawyers Are Everywhere

Lawyers are everywhere—or so it seems. Legally trained individuals work not only in the practice of law, but also in a wide variety of other careers—some related to the law and some seemingly outside of it. In a larger sense, though, in a complex, pluralistic society, there are very few activities that do not have legal implications. Although the legal nexus may be clearer in some areas than in others, it is not an overgeneralization to say that law is everywhere. So it should come as no surprise that lawyers are also everywhere.

We live in a society awash with legal problems, and we are trained in law. How do we apply that legal training in diverse settings where legal problem solving is beneficial? This question assumes that the legal profession is as broad as the fields of endeavor in which legal training is relevant to the resolution of problems and in which lawyers can add value to transactions. Not everyone with legal training applies his or her legal skills in the traditional organizations where

legal services are delivered: law firms, corporate legal departments, and government legal organizations. Viewed most broadly,
nonlegal careers for lawyers may be seen as innovative and novel
systems for delivering legal services outside the framework of the
practicing bar.

In 2000, there were approximately one million lawyers in the
United States. Of these, almost 60 percent worked in private practice, 12.5 percent in business and industry, 12.2 percent for government agencies, including legal and public defenders' offices,
11.4 percent in the judiciary, and 5.1 percent in a variety of other
positions. Only 0.6 percent of the lawyers listed themselves as
retired or inactive. An undetermined percentage of those working
in business and government worked in nonlegal jobs.

A look behind these statistics is revealing. If we assume that the
American Bar Foundation/Martindale figures are accurate, the total
does not include uncounted thousands of lawyers who do not practice law or do not list themselves as lawyers in *Martindale-Hubbell*.
If the vast majority of those who do not appear in *Martindale-Hubbell*
are working, it follows that a great many lawyers work in nonlegal
careers.

The subject of nonlegal careers for lawyers can be viewed in a
larger context, beyond what we normally see as the dividing line
between what is considered "practicing law" and what is not. From
this perspective, the artificial distinctions between traditional
practice and nonlegal careers lose their meaning. Individuals who
get into law school are among the best and brightest of the nation's
college graduates, and those who spend three or four years obtaining a legal education have valuable skills. These skills can be
employed in a variety of settings and can prepare lawyers to compete successfully in the larger employment marketplace.

Dispute Resolution

Traditional legal practice represents one, but not the only, model
under which legal disputes may be resolved. In a competitive marketplace, the most efficient service providers dominate the market

while less efficient providers are weeded out. In the case of legal services, a proliferation of lawyers has increased competition and spawned alternative environments in which legal training may be applied. The broad term *alternative dispute resolution* has become popular among legal educators to describe innovations, such as mediation and arbitration. They represent something different from the adversary process of litigation that most people associate with lawyers. Many people view the adversary system as too cumbersome, time-consuming, costly, and complex to solve the majority of common disputes effectively.

Many alternative forms of dispute resolution operate not only beyond the scope of the judicial system, but outside the sphere of the traditional legal profession. They are, in a word, *nonlegal* alternatives. The point is to keep in mind that you do not have to work in traditional legal position to do legal work or use your legal skills.

Economics

Analysis of lawyer economic surveys suggests a decline in the real income of lawyers who provide "commodity" services. Reports of the disintegration of a number of formerly successful and often prestigious law firms hints at economic Darwinism. Outside the legal profession, a variety of professional service providers seek to compete with lawyers for client business.

At the same time, surveys show that most Americans are not regularly represented by a lawyer, that the majority of people do not seek legal advice until their problems have become irresolvable outside the legal system, and that most people do not use legal assistance in a preventive way. Studies of low-income groups indicate that most are either not represented at all or are underrepresented when dealing with legal problems.

What does all this conflicting evidence mean?

- First, it means that you cannot believe everything you read.
- Second, it means that there are no easy answers.
- Third, it means that all bets are off on who will succeed in the coming decade.

- Fourth, it means that creative entrepreneurial ventures that meet people's need to resolve their legal problems in an effective and economical way will succeed, regardless of whether they are within the traditional legal profession or judicial system.
- Fifth, it means that your legal education can be used to help you excel in the nonlegal field of your choice.
- Sixth, it means that you may find it worthwhile to think outside the box and invest your energy in finding a career that will support you in these challenging times.

Law firms and lawyers have been forced to look at these new economic realities, and the consumers of legal services have had to contend with a proliferation of specialty services. For both lawyers and their clients, changes in society have precipitated changes in the marketplace. (See Gary A. Munneke, *Seize the Future: Forecasting and Influencing the Future of the Legal Profession* [ABA, 2000].)

So What?

When confronted with statistics about the changing profession, one is tempted to ask, So what? Will changes in the demographics of the legal profession, the needs of legal clients, or shifts in the marketplace for professional services have any bearing on me? We hope at least some readers will respond with a resounding "yes," and for those readers, to paraphrase Robert Frost, it may make all the difference.

Defining Nonlegal Careers

3

What Do You Want to Be When You Grow Up?

At the outset, it may be useful to think about the general topic of careers. When you were a child, someone probably asked, "What do you want to be when you grow up?" To which you may have answered "An astronaut!" In high school, you may have attended a career day, where representatives of different professions and businesses came to your school to tell you about their work. In college, conversations with faculty advisors often involved the consideration of careers.

Despite this longstanding emphasis on choosing a career, many people have very little idea about how to define the term. The elusiveness of this concept may contribute to the difficulty that people have in making choices about what to do with their lives. The five-year-old's simplistic vision of the future is a far cry from the law school graduate's complicated decision about what to do with his or her legal training.

A career is more than a series of jobs connected by a common industry. Many workers do not describe themselves as having careers, but rather as having jobs. A job involves doing work, but does not necessarily provide a professional identity. A person with a job may leave work at the end of the day, but one with a career never completely shakes his or her professional identity. After law school you will always be a lawyer, no matter where you are or what you do. Although a career such as law may be established educationally, it may also be developed experientially, over time, through a series of similar or related jobs, or by tenure in and mastery of a single position. In addition, many legal jobs require licensure as a prerequisite to employment, although most nonlegal jobs do not.

The key elements here are skill and identity. Although in a theoretical sense all work requires the application of skills, a career implies the acquisition and application of unique skills shared with those engaged in the same field. Identity denotes a nexus between the skills and the group.

The point is that a career is much more than just a job, or even a series of unconnected jobs. It should have substance, continuity, and direction in order to have meaning. With a career, even if a person holds several different positions over time, they would be connected by common skills and identity, and experience professional growth from basic to more advanced work.

The concepts of work and play are related to careers as well. To work means to earn a living, but for many people it also means the opposite of play. If play is fun, it would seem to follow that work is not fun. But a quick look around confirms that the world is full of people for whom work is not just rewarding or fulfilling, but is actually play. Another way of saying this is that you should seek to get paid for having fun, or at least doing something that gives you pleasure.

If you are not having fun at your work, maybe you should think about doing something else. This does not mean that work is never challenging or difficult, or even sometimes tedious; rather, it means that work can and should be enjoyable. The concept of melding work and play is discussed more fully in subsequent chapters, but it can be said here that this is not an impossible goal.

Who Is a Lawyer?

Careers are often described in terms of groups of people who do similar work, such as professions or trades. Because lawyers are a part of the legal profession, lawyers pursuing nonlegal careers may wonder where they stand in relation to the profession.

A profession is a group of individuals with common education and expertise who provide similar services, maintain some formal system for admission and regulation, and share common values. Traditional professions include law, medicine, ministry, and education. In recent decades many other groups have taken on the mantle of professionalism, perhaps attracted by the greater status, remuneration, and influence held by the traditional professions.

The downside of professional status is that professionals are subject to professional liability when they breach a professional standard of care to their clients and patients. The higher level of skill and knowledge imposes an appropriately higher standard of care in exercising the skill. To prove a violation of the standard of care, a plaintiff must show that the professional's conduct deviated from that of other similarly situated professionals, based on custom and usage in the profession. Thus, in law, professional conduct involves a greater duty or higher standard of care than would be required of the nonprofessional.

The question is sometimes asked whether the legal profession comprises those persons who actually practice law, those who are licensed to do so, or those who have graduated from law school. A second consideration is whether those who have been educated as lawyers but do not practice law should be held to the standards of practicing lawyers.

By the narrowest definition, the legal profession includes those who practice law by providing legal services to others. Arguably, this definition would exclude judges, lawyer-legislators, law professors, legally trained law librarians, and many others who are commonly perceived as part of the legal profession. Many lawyers engaged in completely nonlegal activities still think of themselves as members of the legal profession who simply happen to be pursuing other activities at the time. In fact, there is considerable movement back and forth across the line between practicing law and engaging in extrinsic activities, so this narrow definition of the legal profession seems unnecessarily limited.

Drawing the line at the point of licensure makes for an easy demarcation but presents its own problems. Licensure limits only who may represent clients in court and give purely legal advice, but much law-related work is performed by those who are not licensed to practice law. Someone who has not been to law school may engage in the same legally related activities as someone else who has graduated from law school. It is arguable that the legally trained person is more proficient at handling legal issues than someone who lacks legal training. In fact, a considerable amount of legal work is handled by law graduates who are not licensed to practice in the jurisdiction in which they work. Thus, using licensure as a criterion for the legal profession also has its limitations.

Although some may quarrel, the term *legal profession* as used in this book refers to all those who have graduated from law school, regardless of whether they are formally licensed or are engaged in the practice of law. Because the scope of legally related services extends far beyond the limits of the formal organized bar, and because many lawyers actively provide these services, it makes sense to define the legal profession as broadly as possible. Conceptually, there is a bright line between those who have graduated from law school and those who have not. Defining the legal profession as the universe of law school graduates allows for the recognition of a subset of licensed lawyers, containing a subset of practicing lawyers (Chart 1). Because law school graduates will always be able to use their legal training, it follows that they will exercise their legal skills in whatever work they do. Therefore, this book deals with all lawyers except those in the subset of practicing lawyers.

This approach avoids the rather artificial distinction between law-related and nonlegal work. The preceding discussion should make clear that lawyers apply legal skills to virtually every occupation they pursue. Indeed, it is difficult to imagine a line of work where legal training would not be an asset. Law-related work includes activities for which legal skills are regularly used and for which legal training provides an advantage. The problem with this

Chart 1
The Universe of the Legal Profession

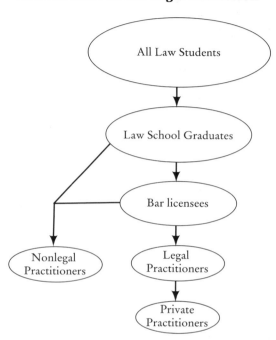

dichotomy is that it is a futile exercise in line drawing that ultimately contributes little to an understanding of legal careers.

Undoubtedly, some types of work require more legal skills than others and some lines of work are more closely associated with the practice of law than others. Can it be said, however, that a legislative aide does not use her legal skills? Or that legal training does not help a professional baseball manager in his job? Or that someone engaged in volunteer community service is not applying legal skills on a regular basis?

In actuality, lawyers tend to legalize whatever they touch. Although critics of the legal profession decry this phenomenon, it is arguable that legal analysis and a legal approach to solving problems enhance the dispute resolution process.

Regardless of your view of the merit of this legalization, there is little doubt that it is occurring. And, because the profession has chosen not to limit the number of lawyers, it is inevitable that lawyers will move into other fields in significant numbers. Legal training itself is so broad that it should not be surprising to find lawyers who are writers, business chief executive officers, news reporters, certified public accountants (CPAs), labor organizers, engineers, scientists, teachers, and just about everything else imaginable.

Often, lawyers in fields outside the practice of law must possess or develop skills beyond those required for the practice of law. Consequently, dual degrees, nonlegal work experience, and contacts outside of the legal profession may be valuable or necessary to succeed in a nonlegal career. In a world where legal issues permeate every form of human endeavor, those who are trained as lawyers have much to offer, whatever vocation they pursue.

Jobs and Careers

There is a myth in the legal profession that lawyers keep one job throughout their legal careers. If this myth was ever true, which is debatable, it certainly is not today. The average lawyer will hold four to eight jobs in the forty years between law school graduation and retirement, and a high percentage of lawyers will make at least one major career change in their lives.

In *Working*, Studs Terkel, a lawyer himself, suggests that job dissatisfaction is pervasive in our society. People do not seem to be happy in their present positions; they are all on the road to somewhere and just passing time in their current jobs.

Lawyers considering alternative careers are not alone. It would be unwise, however, to assume that dissatisfaction in the legal profession is just due to our changing times, or caused by sunspot activity, or some other global witchcraft.

In many ways the legal profession is unique. The dissatisfaction of lawyers with their professional lives can be explained, if not totally understood. One reason may be that there are so many alternative careers available to dissatisfied lawyers. Also, a caveat is in order. Dissatisfaction inspires progress, feeds careers, and builds futures. Each of us, in one sense, is always in the job market.

There are very few people who would not leave what they are doing for some golden opportunity.

When we experience dissatisfaction in our work, we have three options:

◆ Change ourselves,
◆ Change our environment, or
◆ Leave the environment.

When we change ourselves we accept whatever it was that was bothering us. When we change the environment, we eliminate the offending problem. If we cannot do that, we leave the environment and look for something new. Sometimes we decide for ourselves to make changes in our professional lives, and sometimes we are forced to change. If a lawyer is told he will not be made a partner in his law firm but can stay as an associate, he can accept the decision, attempt to prove that he should be made partner, or pull out his old résumé and begin to update it. (See John L. Holland, *Making Vocational Choices.*)

Career decisions are almost always complex, and involve many considerations. Factors such as employability in the marketplace, tolerance for the present situation, attractiveness of new opportunities, willingness to assume a risk, and need for security inevitably weigh heavily in the equation. Every year thousands of lawyers change jobs, and thousands of people enter law school with the idea that legal education is a path to career change. For some, the transition is smooth, but for others change is difficult and painful. Sometimes it is destructive.

Success is more than blind luck. When we succeed, we frequently use the same skills that helped us to succeed in the past. In other words, changing careers ought to involve careful evaluation of past job behavior to determine competencies that will most likely produce success in a new situation.

Feeling that a job contributes to a positive direction in your career is essential to your self-esteem and job satisfaction. Jobs perceived as dead ends or as unchallenging usually become former jobs for those who can neither change them nor accept the status quo. For some people, salary can influence whether a job is considered to have a future. For others, it is the opportunity for skill development and other types of rewards that are important. A low-paying but psychologically rewarding job is more likely to be perceived as lacking a future than a high-paying but mindless one.

New lawyers experience the greatest levels of dissatisfaction in the first one to two years of practice, but satisfaction increases over time, as they gain experience. Sometimes legally trained individuals express frustration with their work, and many leave the practice of law as a result. It is important to realize that frustration is a natural part of the transition from law school to law practice, from an educational setting mastered over twenty or more years, to a work environment that is often radically new. This transitional anxiety normally subsides after three to five years, as the new lawyer masters the craft.

Some lawyers, however, remain disenchanted with legal work. It is not fulfilling for them. Often, these individuals have made career choices inconsistent with their professional skills or work values. Their disquietude could have been predicted before they went to work.

What these unhappy lawyers often fail to realize is that, although they may be dissatisfied with their current situation, there may be other places where they can use their legal skills and achieve satisfaction. They also fail to recognize that the limits of private practice are not a boundary to the application of legal skills.

Building on Experience

Students and lawyers contemplating a nonlegal career need to adopt a mind-set that recognizes the contributions of all their experiences, both legal and nonlegal, in making them unique professionals. Just as many law students pursuing legal careers ignore their nonlegal experiences when they consider career options, those who pursue nonlegal careers often forget the important skills they have derived from a legal education.

It may be difficult for those who did not enjoy the law school experience to look back with objectivity on the positive aspects of legal education. They may have trouble recognizing the array of skills that they acquired and honed while in law school, such as research skills, the art of persuasion, and analytical ability. Yet, the truth is that legal education prepares law students not just for the practice of law but for a wide variety of other careers, and the skills gained in law school are transferable into many other fields of endeavor. In addition, substantive legal knowledge can come in handy. Practically speaking, if two candidates are otherwise roughly equal in the eyes of a potential employer, the fact that one of them has a legal education may tip the hiring decision in the direction of the law graduate.

As a general proposition, everyone should look at all their experiences when thinking about careers, preparing résumés, contacting employers about openings, and interviewing for positions. It is critical to success in these efforts to view yourself apart from the pack, as a unique individual with special skills and abilities.

A Variety of Careers for Lawyers

The number of careers open to persons trained in the law is almost unlimited. There are legal considerations in every form of human endeavor in this complex world. Even when the work is not practicing law in the sense of giving legal advice to clients, a lawyer working in a field outside the law deals with the interface between legal skills and another field. Legal skills, such as spotting issues, analyzing problems, conducting research, and persuading others, undoubtedly give the lawyer an ability to manage this exchange effectively.

Lawyers who do not practice law are often described as working in nontraditional or alternative careers. This terminology is unfortunate because it implies that these positions are second-rate. Throughout this book, the term *nonlegal careers* is used in reference to careers that fall outside the practice of law and the term *alternative* is used to suggest two or more possible choices.

Those who wonder whether law practice will be satisfying for them, or who no longer feel excited about their legal jobs, should ask, Can my skills be better used in a different field? If the answer is "yes," or even "very possibly," it might be time to consider something new.

Any career decision has both pros and cons. Because your needs, interests, and abilities do not duplicate those of any other person, it is vitally important that you give careful consideration to all the factors that might bear upon your success.

In light of the sheer number of possibilities open to you, as well as the expectation that the number can be expected to increase in the future, there is obviously considerable opportunity here. American ingenuity has created a host of organizations where legal knowledge has effective application. There are also many opportunities in entrepreneurial ventures. This range of choices maximizes the possibility of matching your particular talents and skills to specific opportunities. This, in turn increases your chances of finding career satisfaction.

Another consideration is the fact that nonlegal skills may prove to be more portable than a law license. Alternatively, if you wish to confine your job search to a specific geographic area, this portability works to your advantage by increasing the number of possible employers.

Taking the Bar

A final consideration may be very difficult to assess simply because it involves looking into the future and projecting your anticipated career path at a time when you do not have all the information you need to make a decision. You need to decide whether you wish to be admitted to the bar. In most nonlegal positions, bar admission is not essential to take full advantage of the skills you have already acquired from law school training. On the other hand, admission might be important for future promotion because of additional responsibilities you might perform or pay grades you might be entitled to earn. There is no easy answer to this question, but from the standpoint of flexibility bar admission is a definite advantage.

The National Conference of Bar Examiners publishes information on admission requirements, both for recent graduates and lawyers already licensed in at least one jurisdiction, and BAR/BRI publishes an annual *Bar Review Digest* that summarizes these requirements. You can also go directly to the Board of Law Examiners in any state to which you are thinking about relocating to request information and application forms for that state. Most law schools provide bar applications for the state where they are located and other states where a substantial number of graduates settle. For both new and licensed lawyers, it is important to make inquiries about bar admission requirements early, to avoid problems in the application process (see **www.ncbex.org**).

Why mention this consideration in a book on nonlegal careers? Whether you ever practice law or not, it is generally a good idea to obtain your law license. If you think you might ever return from a nonlegal career to the practice of law, you certainly will want to take the bar as soon after law school as possible, rather than coming back after several years. For licensed lawyers, some states limit the number of years a lawyer may maintain inactive status without being required to take the entire exam afresh. Even if you decide not to take the bar exam, make an affirmative decision about what you want to do rather than a decision by default.

Starting Over Again

The law school graduate who chooses not to practice law must recognize the strong possibility that it may be difficult after a few years to second-guess the decision. The reason is both economic and psychological. The psychological side is fairly simple: once you are established in another profession or industry, you develop contacts, gain experiences, and acculturate to the mores of the alternative career. Economically, as you earn raises beyond entry level, you may reach the point at which you cannot afford to go back to practice law.

Lawyers who take time out for parental leave or other reasons may find that classmates who started out with them have moved up the ladder, not only in experience and responsibility, but also in pay and status. Even part-time lawyers may discover that their lifestyle choices retard their professional development. It is not a question of whether making these choices is desirable—there are pros and cons to every career decision—it is the reality that all decisions have consequences. One of the vérités of career development is that there is a cost to taking time out from the practice of law, which at some point may make reentry prohibitively expensive, both figuratively and literally.

Because the choice of whether to pursue a nonlegal career is a major one, it deserves your most thoughtful consideration. Even at the start, your choices determine the approach you take to the marketplace now and in the future.

▼▼▼▼▼

Christine joined a corporation as a compliance officer. Her classmate, Elena, went to work for the legal department of the same company. Both Christine and Elena passed the bar before starting to work for the company, and both gained highly specialized training in the specialized procedures, problems, and policies of their respective departments; both used their law degrees every day at work. Over time, Christine and Elena took on greater responsibilities and received periodic increases in salary. After five years, however, if the two friends decided to trade jobs, each would find themselves as entry-level workers with limited experience, earning entry-level pay.

When to Choose a Nonlegal Career

4

Not everyone opts to pursue a nonlegal career at the same stage of professional development. This chapter examines three entry points: before law school, during law school, and after law school. You may want to skip to the section that best fits your personal situation.

Before Law School

Many of those who pursue nonlegal careers either make the decision to eschew the practice of law or are predisposed to do so before they arrive at first-year orientation. Most, but not all, of these students pursue a legal education on a part-time basis while continuing their nonlegal employment. These people, who come to law school to make a career change, do so for a variety of disparate reasons:

- ◆ A number of students enter law school with no intention of practicing law. Some elect to remain in the nonlegal career that they pursued before law school. Many students however, decide to stay where they are after examining and rejecting career choices in the traditional legal arena.

- Some are unhappy in their present work; they believe they are in a job and not a career; their nonlegal work was merely a way to finance a legal education; or they may articulate any number of other reasons. These students decide to pursue the study of law precisely because they do not want to do something else. Although they may bring with them certain skills from their nonlegal employment, some mistakenly think they are essentially abandoning one career path and starting another. In the game of life, they are returning to square one.

- Other students view a law degree as an opportunity to grow in a field or company where they are already employed. They may want to move into a legal or patent department or use their legal skills in their current job. The employer may provide salary enhancements for employees who earn advanced degrees.

- Still others have dreamed of attending law school for years but became sidetracked with work and family responsibilities until reaching a point in life where they could pursue their youthful objective. Many of these people are firmly ensconced in other careers and view law as a part-time avocation, or even a postretirement second career.

- A final group may develop an interest in the law as a result of something unconnected to work, such as becoming an addict of the television show *Law and Order* or being intrigued by a legal case in which they are personally involved, such as probating Uncle Harry's will. For these aspiring lawyers, it may be the study of law rather than the practice of law that leads them to law school.

Ideally, a career should build upon past accomplishments. A career change should reflect a transition rather than an abrupt move from one unrelated field to another. An analogy might be the building of a pyramid. Each level of the pyramid rests upon the blocks in the level below, gradually ascending to the apex (see Chart 2). If the builder laid the first level of blocks, and then began

Chart 2
Building on Experience

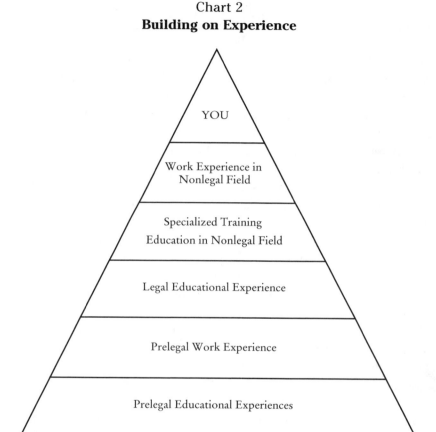

to build on just one side, the pyramid would never be completed. The new construction would require more effort just to get back to the first level of the pyramid. To be successful, the builder must move up one level at a time.

Similarly, the law student who uses legal skills to enhance a prelegal career is building a career pyramid, whereas the student who jettisons a prelegal career is going back to start another foundation. Viewed in this light, it is a wise student who comes to law school planning to continue or enhance a nonlegal career through law. Also wise is the student with a unique background who is hoping to meld his or her prelegal work experience with law.

Several problems face the law student contemplating a return to a prelegal career. The first involves family and friends who ask, "If you want to continue to do what you did before, why are you going to law school?" They may not understand about pyramids and career development. To the extent that you must explain your actions to these well-wishers, you will have to clarify your reasons in your own mind. Such clarification can be useful, but the explanation itself may be difficult.

A second but related problem is an internal one: your own self-doubts about choosing a path that goes against the grain of the majority of your classmates. Most people who come to law school plan to practice law, and most who graduate do. You must possess enough self-confidence to know that it is not necessary to follow the crowd. In short, you need to exercise considerable honesty and self-knowledge in your own decision making.

A third, more pragmatic, problem is that legal and nonlegal careers may not be easy to integrate. Just as it may not make sense to turn your back on nonlegal experience, it would be an exercise in futility to go to law school and never use your legal training. What you must determine is how you can apply your legal skills in the nonlegal setting. As noted in the previous chapter, legal training can enhance the skills of practitioners in almost any field.

The task of maximizing the benefit of a legal education in a nonlegal career path may be challenging or even formidable. So, if you decide to stay in a nonlegal career, you should give careful consideration to how you will use your training as a lawyer.

The final problem involves those who continue to practice in a prelegal career: They may price themselves out of a legal career. Starting to work as an entry-level lawyer may require a salary cut. Those who have risen on the career ladder in another field and assumed a lifestyle commensurate with their status at work may face a difficult decision about starting over.

It is not uncommon for such individuals to maintain their legal skills while working part time or *pro bono* as a lawyer and then to practice law full time after retirement from their first careers. Good pensions can provide the cushions necessary to let them pursue law at an entry level. Those who started work in their early twenties may be looking at retirement in their mid-forties to early fifties, leaving lots of time to practice law.

Some fields, such as law and accounting, lend themselves to what is called *dual practice,* in which the individual pursues both professions simultaneously. Although a dual practice may present ethical problems related to conflicts of interest and solicitation of business, such an arrangement represents a viable path for law graduates who do not want to give up their prelegal careers.

During Law School

In contrast to those who come to law school with a strong predisposition to follow a nonlegal career, many law students enter law school with no preconceived idea about what they want to do after graduation. Either they are not certain what the opportunities really are, or they are naturally open-minded about the possibilities. Whatever the reasons, students who choose nonlegal careers begin to look at nonlegal alternatives as a part of the career planning process in law school. In fact, many students begin law school with no preconceived ideas regarding the disability of pursuing a legal versus a nonlegal career.

Some students may assume they will practice law when they graduate until they begin to explore what lawyers actually do. They recognize that their career opportunities are not limited by the narrow bounds of the practice of law. How do they begin to consider nonlegal career opportunities? Usually, something happens to open their eyes to alternative careers: a work experience, a law school panel, a conversation with a career advisor or professor, or reading this book.

When students reach a point in the educational process where they really do not want to become practicing lawyers, or at least are not committed to a traditional legal career, they naturally begin to explore opportunities outside the legal arena. This enlightenment may come as a shock to parents, spouses, partners, or friends. Unfortunately, too many people do not act on the revelation that they do not want to practice law and enter a legal career that ultimately proves unsatisfying. In the annals of dissatisfied lawyers who quit the practice of law, it is interesting to speculate who among them could have seen it coming.

Chart 3

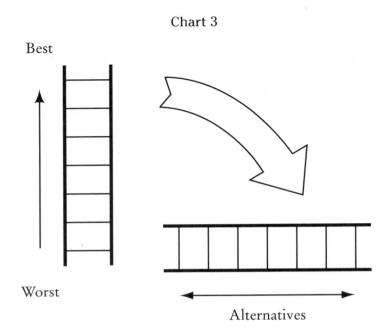

The simple solution is that students planning to attend law school should not limit themselves in their career options. Too often, law students perceive a career as a ladder, with a job at a prestigious large law firm at the top and a nonlegal career at the bottom. They view the job search process as climbing up the ladder as high as they can reach and holding on.

In actuality, the ladder should be viewed horizontally with the rungs representing options (Chart 3). According to this paradigm, different options are best suited to different people, but no option is intrinsically superior to any other. Adopting this simple conceptual device can save you a lot of heartache in life, because turning the ladder on its side increases your options.

Although National Association for Law Placement statistics suggest that almost all of those who want legal employment and who obtain the proper licensing eventually will find it, the reality is that a small percentage of graduates will enter the nonlegal field by default. Some law school graduates pursue nonlegal careers because their opportunities in the legal field are limited. Some have unrealistically rigid requirements for employment; some become frustrated with the legal job market and extend their search to nonlegal areas; and a small number do not pass the bar. These individuals need to put a positive spin on events and go forward with the rest of their lives.

At least some law school graduates will accept nonlegal jobs for a period of time before they find legal work. Practicing lawyers may take jobs in nonlegal fields between legal jobs or as a sort of sabbatical from the practice of law while they decide what to do with their lives. For these people, a nonlegal job is part of a career transition but not necessarily a long-term commitment. Ideally, nonlegal employment should complement a larger career pattern in a lawyer's life, but this is not always possible. A nonlegal job may be more a means of putting food on the table than achieving long-term career goals. Such individuals will find this book useful even if they consider their foray into the nonlegal arena to be a temporary one.

After Law School

Lawyers who decide to pursue a nonlegal career as an alternative to the practice of law represent a much larger group. These lawyers enter a nonlegal career after working in a traditional area of law practice. Among those who choose a nonlegal career after law school, a substantial number move into an area in which they have prior experience. A smaller number embark on an entirely new career. Those who leave the practice of law include lawyers who become disenchanted with purely legal work, those who become involved in activities outside the practice of law, often through contacts with clients, and lawyers who retire after a career of practicing law but choose to continue to work in some other area.

You will need to examine your skills, what led you to make this change, and how to strike a balance between the benefits of your present career and the risks of a career change. You may need to invest in additional training or education. For example, if you want to join a CPA firm—and CPA firms hire a significant number of lawyers—and you have an undergraduate accounting degree but never passed the CPA exam, you may want to go back and take that exam. On the other hand, if you are a history major but want to pursue a career in accounting, you may want to consider getting a masters in accounting and then taking the CPA exam. Why? Because your opportunities in the CPA firm are greater if you have your CPA license than if you are only licensed as a lawyer.

The number of graduates who enter nonlegal careers after law school is difficult to gauge because there are no reliable surveys that measure the patterns of career change for lawyers. Anecdotally, career advisors, headhunters, and students of the legal profession estimate the number of mid- and late-career shifts into nonlegal areas can recount endless stories of defections from the law. Informal evidence based on the number of lawyers who drop their bar membership each year suggest that these numbers are substantial. It is probable that the lawyers who leave the practice of law after some time, in contrast to those who decide to pursue a nonlegal career before or during law school, experience a greater degree of dissatisfaction with practice than those who never enter the world of law practice.

Making the Choice

The bottom line is that practicing law is not for everyone. Whether they reach this conclusion before, during, or after law school, a significant segment of the legally educated population finds work outside the law. This book is a useful tool regardless of when one enters the nonlegal job market and whether the move is temporary or permanent. Those law students and graduates who require more detailed assistance with the process of making career choices, and those who are contemplating both legal and nonlegal careers, should also read and use *The Legal Career Guide: From Law Student to Lawyer* by Gary A. Munneke (ABA Career Series, 2002). Lawyers who have already graduated should consider looking at *Changing Jobs: A Handbook for Lawyers in the New Millennium,* edited by Heidi McNeil Staudenmaier (ABA, 1999). Of particular interest to women law students and graduates is *Women-at-Law: Lessons Learned Along the Pathways to Success,* by Phyllis Horn Epstein (ABA, 2004).

Just as practicing law is not for everyone, neither is a nonlegal career. Looking at the universe of legally trained individuals, who is best suited for nonlegal work? Who is most likely to succeed and find satisfaction outside the practice of law? The answer is not an easy one, but there are a few clues:

♦ Skills—Most nonlegal careers require their own special skills. These may include understanding a technical language, knowing unique procedures, appreciating professional values of the nonlegal field, and using special training on the job. If a lawyer does not have these skills at the outset, he or she must find a way to develop them (for example, a lawyer who decides to become a librarian may need to obtain a professional library degree as well as practical experience working in a library before moving up the career ladder in the library field). Although these skills can be developed before, during, or after law school, they are almost always a prerequisite for success. Put another way, legal training alone is seldom enough.

♦ Values—The less one's identity is subsumed in the professional identity of a lawyer, the easier it is to leave the law. Practicing lawyers as a group share some basic values about representing clients zealously, advocating positions, and protecting confidential information, to name a few. These values are taught in law school, nurtured in practice, and sustained by the disciplinary system. Although not all lawyers agree completely on questions involving interpretation, there is a kind of internal cohesiveness in these values that manifests itself in a shared professional identity. This does not mean that a lawyer who pursues a nonlegal career will not take many lawyerly values with her to a new occupation; it simply means that her sense of self-worth does not depend on being a lawyer.

♦ Self-image—Lawyers who leave the traditional legal profession may sacrifice some built-in support groups available to those who pursue traditional career paths. Families may not understand the choice. The law school community may not appreciate or understand why a student deviates from the traditional career path. Classmates and other lawyers may feel threatened or abandoned by a colleague's decision to work outside the practice of law. Thus, someone who embarks on a nonlegal career must have a strong internal sense of identity. He must be resourceful, independent, and even a little iconoclastic.

◆ Network—Those who have spent considerable time around law students and lawyers may find that their contacts outside the traditional legal profession are limited. The longer they work in the practice of law, the more problematic this difficulty can become. Those who wish to pursue a nonlegal career must find ways to maintain lines of communication with people in the area of their nonlegal interest. This is somewhat easier for lawyers who come to law school with a preexisting nonlegal career, or who maintain contacts with nonlegal areas through clients. Many lawyers, however, find that they are cut off from information about opportunities because they do not have contacts outside the bar. You can address this particular dilemma by developing and maintaining a network in an area of professional interest outside the law. This can be accomplished through membership in industry-specific organizations, volunteering for work in your area of interest, and reading specific journals, visiting Web sites, and exploring other resources.

◆ Dreams—No one ever completely escapes that childhood question, "What do you want to be when you grow up?" As long as the answer to this question is "a practicing lawyer," it will be difficult to find satisfaction outside the practice of law. Similarly, if the answer to the question has never been "a practicing lawyer," it will be difficult to find happiness within. An honest self-appraisal focusing on your fundamental aspirations in life is useful, and, as simple as it sounds, the person who chooses a nonlegal career because that is what she wants to do (or who she wants to be) is the person most likely to succeed in that arena.

It is clear that law school-educated professional make the choice to pursue a nonlegal career for a variety of reasons at different times in their lives. The choice involves a number of complex decisions that may not be easy to make. There is no penalty for exploring alternatives, and in one sense the only way you can really come face to face with a life choice such as this is to create the proverbial fork in the road.

The Skills You Offer

5

Applicants for positions may feel that the qualities employers seek present an impenetrable mystery. This simply is not so. With a little imagination and some practice, you can understand the qualifications required for any position. You should be able to analyze the requirements by asking only four basic questions: Will the position require any specific legal skills? What degree of education is required for the nonlegal field you hope to enter? What personal qualities are required, and are they desirable? And what industry-specific knowledge and procedural know-how is required for you to fill the demands of the position successfully?

Legal Skills

The first question you might ask is whether there are any skills that might be acceptable substitutes for the specified technical expertise. Are there related skills that might enhance job performance? Legal training might provide basic skills that would be useful in this work, and you may have enhanced those skills if you happened to have concentrated your studies in real estate and related fields. Take a look at the ten fundamental lawyering skills identified in the ABA's Report on Law Schools and the Profession: Narrowing the Gap (The MacCrate Report), and think about how these skills might be used in the nonlegal work you are considering:

- Problem Solving
- Legal Analysis and Reasoning
- Legal Research
- Factual Investigation
- Communication
- Counseling
- Negotiation
- Litigation and Alternative Dispute Resolution
- Organization and Management of Legal Work
- Recognizing and Resolving Ethical Dilemmas

This list should be viewed as exemplary rather than exhaustive. Think about other skills you may have developed before and during law school, both in legal and other environments. If you have already graduated from law school, consider the experiences that have built additional skills, particularly transferable ones, since graduation. Now, imagine ways that these skills might be employed in the nonlegal field of your choice.

By analyzing your own experience and training, you can pinpoint those skills you have acquired that would put you ahead of the competition. An analysis may also serve to eliminate consideration of certain paths for which you do not have the necessary technical background.

Many skills are transferable—that is, portable from one occupation to another. Too often, those seeking employment describe their skills in job-specific terms. If they view their legal skills as transferable and then translate those skills into the language of the new field, they will have overcome a major hurdle in finding a nonlegal job.

Educational Requirements

When a business organization is seeking to employ someone for its legal department, it is obvious that a law degree is required, simply because bar admission is basic to the job. Most nonlegal positions, however, do not specifically call for a law degree, yet a law degree may help you even if a J.D. is not required for the job. It then becomes your task to convince the employer why a law degree qualifies you and sets you apart from others for the position you seek.

If you have not had much experience with the job search process, you may want to read *The Legal Career Guide: From Law Student to Lawyer* (ABA, 2002), by Gary A. Munneke, for suggestions on analyzing your skills. Chapter 6 of this book discusses conducting a job search in a nonlegal area and offers suggestions on how to sell your law degree to potential employers.

Personal Attributes

Assume that leadership potential and the ability to work effectively with others are prime qualifications necessary for success in any professional position. Every organization is seeking candidates with these characteristics. These transferable personal attributes may be as critical to nonlegal employers as skills and education, so it makes sense to understand your intangible strengths:

- Initiative
- Ability to plan
- Adaptability
- Versatility
- Ability to concentrate
- Decisiveness
- Ability to express oneself
- Motivation
- Creativity
- Innovation

Just as in the case of skills, this list is not exhaustive. You might attempt to define additional qualities that will contribute to success in the nonlegal setting. All of these attributes contribute to successful job performance. At this point, however, you need to isolate those traits that are most conducive to performance in a specific area. For example, you might determine that originality and creativity are more important to the marketing function than to contract administration. After you have done research and identified the qualities needed, analyze your own personal strengths in the area that you are considering and assess your competitive status as a candidate.

Knowledge of Nonlegal Industries

If you are just entering the business world, the employer may not expect you to have specific knowledge about a particular market segment or business practice. It may not be something you can learn by taking certain courses in school, but you learn by on-the-job experience. On the other hand, if you do possess expertise in the nonlegal field, your background may prove to be a decided advantage.

The importance of this last question as you begin a nonlegal-career search is that the answer may define the type of position that you are seeking. If you do not possess a solid background in a field you are considering, you may find that employers will want to consider you for a general entry-level position. The most common title given to this post in the corporate world is management trainee, and that is precisely what you would be.

Management trainees are trained by management in the industry knowledge and procedural know-how required for more-advanced positions. Government or other organizations may prefer to use the title intern. In a few industries there are specific titles for entry-level positions, such as claims adjuster in the insurance industry. Despite the variety of titles, the general principle of learning the business on the job still applies.

◆ Knowledge of the law—Legal training and experience provide tools to help your job performance in the nonlegal setting because every type of business involves law at some level. If the organization you work for enters into contract or other legal transaction, you may be able to understand what the contract or transaction requires of the parties in a special way that nonlawyers do not. Having this type of knowledge may help to make a legally trained person successful in a nonlegal position.

◆ Analytical ability—Legal educators often talk about "learning to think like a lawyer." Do not take this ability for granted. It was pounded into you in three or four years of law school training until it became ingrained and second nature. Critical thinking is a skill that applies itself easily to all types of situations, not just legal cases. It is not a common skill, as you will discover when you deal with people who cannot see the forest for the trees and with others who cannot see the trees for the forest!

◆ Problem-solving ability—The old adage "If anything can go wrong, it will," sometimes referred to as Murphy's Law, is commonplace in the business community. The ability to solve problems and suggest remedies is a highly valued quality, involving a number of legal skills. Furthermore, these skills are not easily acquired, as no doubt your own memories of law school will attest.

◆ Persuasiveness—Essentially, this skill involves marshaling your facts in a logical and orderly manner to persuade someone of the soundness of your conclusions. In any given situation, you have a number of facts and supporting data. Consider the different ways you would present these facts to a client whom you were counseling, as a defense lawyer in a jury trial, or in an appellate brief. This persuasive skill is just as valuable in the business community and increases in value as you move up in it.

◆ Self-confidence—Through the ritual of being called on by professors to discuss cases and being challenged to defend your responses, you have learned to listen critically, hold your ground, and respond logically. You may not fully appreciate the value of this talent until you enter the business world. If you have learned one thing in law school, it is that you express your thoughts confidentially in difficult situations.

Although it is possible to describe common skills, no two lawyers have exactly the same set of skills. It is important to recognize skills held in common with other legally-trained individuals, but unique personal skills are just as important in the transition to a new environment.

Finding a Job in a Nonlegal Career 6

An Overview of the Process

The task of finding a job in a nonlegal career is part of the larger career planning process. It is a simple axiom that a person must know what he is looking for if he expects to find it. The following chart may help to place the nonlegal career search in perspective. There are two basic processes in career planning: the career-choice process and the job search process. The career-choice process, which comes first, involves making decisions about what you want to do. The job search process, as the name suggests, involves actualizing the plan by finding a job. Although career planning is sometimes viewed as a sequence of steps directed at obtaining employment, it should be regarded as a life-long activity. In other words, you should always be evaluating your career plans and considering new opportunities.

Chart 4
Munneke's Pyramid—Overview of the Process

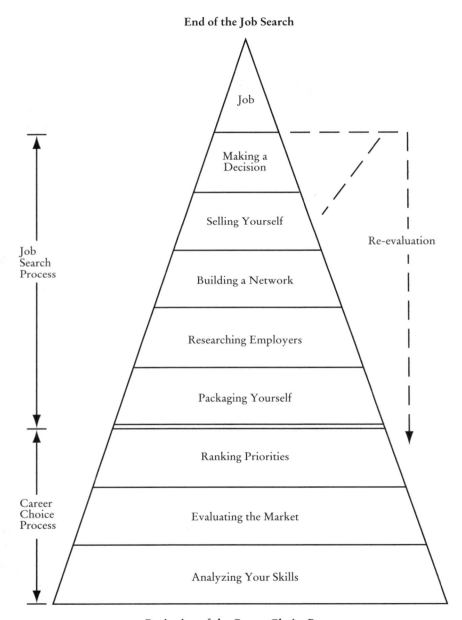

End of the Job Search

Job

Making a
Decision

Selling Yourself

Re-evaluation

Building a Network

Job
Search
Process

Researching Employers

Packaging Yourself

Ranking Priorities

Career
Choice
Process

Evaluating the Market

Analyzing Your Skills

Beginning of the Career Choice Process

The career-choice process involves filtering a great deal of information into a manageable database, analyzing the data, and drawing conclusions from it. There are three basic steps in this process:

- ◆ Skills assessment—The first thing you must do is figure out what you do well. You can do this by looking at your past experiences to identify what will make you marketable to employers (see Chapter 5). A basic assumption is that you will be happier doing something that you do well than an activity you do poorly. Another area of exploration involves the identification of personal work values involving your morals, politics, coworkers, and physical surroundings that make up your work environment, which may be critical to career satisfaction and professional growth.
- ◆ Market assessment—The next step is to evaluate the market. This analysis involves collecting information about potential careers and making realistic assessments about opportunities. Some possibilities that sound good when you first consider them may prove to be less than viable. In contrast to personal skills, values, and interests, the marketplace of career alternatives is volatile.
- ◆ Goals assessment—This step of the process involves synthesizing the conclusions drawn from the previous two steps into a set of working priorities. The aim is not to reach a single rigid goal (for example, to be president of the United States in twenty years), but rather to create a flexible, ordered list that will define the parameters of the job search.

In general, the career-choice process precedes the job search process, which also contains a number of steps. This process is more likely to be fruitful if you proceed through these steps in order:

- ◆ Advance preparation—The first thing you will need is a good résumé. Résumés in nonlegal areas may look different than standard résumés for purely legal jobs. This subject is covered in greater detail later in this chapter. In addition, depending on the industry, you may need writing samples, transcripts, letters of recommendation, or special licenses. Find out what the industry standard is, and follow it. (See "Your Résumé," page 46 in this chapter.)

◆ Networking—The stronger your network of contacts in the nonlegal field you wish to pursue, the better your chances of finding a job. The subject of building a network is covered more fully in *The Legal Career Guide,* but a few basic points can be made here. First, there is no magic involved in networking. It is simply making contacts with professional people who share interests or needs. Second, you do not need to be born with contacts. Networking means going out and meeting people and developing professional relationships. Third, networking is more than a list of names. For a network to work, it must be massaged, and communication must be regular and meaningful. Fourth, networking is a two-way street. If you are perceived as someone who only calls when you need something, or never give anything to others, your network can damage you professionally instead of helping you.

◆ Researching employers—Although you will have collected considerable information about employers during the career-choice process, you still need to conduct specific research on potential employers and openings before contacting them. The more you know about an employer, the better your chances of being hired. The more generic your knowledge of the employer, the less likely you are to get the job. What sounds simple in actuality takes discipline and determination to dig up the information you need. General information about a variety of nonlegal careers is covered in Chapters 7–14, while specific pointers on contacting nonlegal employers are presented later in this chapter.

◆ Marketing yourself—If you think in terms of selling yourself, then contacting potential buyers and selling the product through interviews is the linchpin of the entire process. Just as it is unwise to start selling yourself without doing the necessary homework, it does no good to do your homework and then do a poor job of selling yourself.

If you follow this model, you will improve your chances of a successful job search tremendously. Part of the challenge will be to convince your potential employer that you are committed to your new nonlegal career and that your law degree does not leave you overqualified for the job.

Nevertheless, there are no guarantees. You can follow all the advice in this book and still come up empty-handed. The decisions you make may not prove to be the best ones for you in the long run. You may need to reevaluate your priorities and search plans based on your actual experience in the job market. This is an imprecise art, not an exact science.

In making a decision to pursue a nonlegal career, do not forget the following principles mentioned earlier in this book. Although these may also apply to the legal career search, they take on special meaning in nonlegal fields.

- ◆ Alternatives—What are the alternatives? Are they realistic? Can you get from here to there? It is important to make sure that you always have more than one option. Although your choices should be prioritized, you should never reach the point where you have only one option—or worse, none.
- ◆ Burning bridges—Career planning inherently involves foreclosing some options by making other choices. This may be difficult for some people whose lives prior to law school have involved keeping open as many options as possible.
- ◆ Focus—Because the nonlegal job market is so much more extensive than the legal market, it is easy to lose focus—to try to boil the ocean. You have limited time and energy, so you should make the most of both commodities.

By now you probably realize that obtaining a nonlegal position that will allow you to use the skills you acquired in law school requires a different approach than you would use if you were seeking a position in legal practice. In both areas, however, more positions are probably lost through failure to do adequate homework than for any other reason.

Think of the hard work you have put in obtaining a legal education, not to mention the financial burdens you have shouldered.

It is worth an additional investment of your time, effort, and money to find the type of work you want. Besides, it is your search, and no one can do it as well as you.

Your Résumé

You need to develop a résumé. Too many people put the cart before the horse. They want to start writing the résumé before they have analyzed their qualifications and the qualifications needed for the industry they decide to approach. This is particularly important in approaching the business community, as opposed to the legal community. In contrast to the law office for which your legal education and experience may be of singular interest, the completion of a legal education is only one of a number of qualifications you bring to a nonlegal organization.

The nonlegal organization will want to know about other aspects of your education and training that are pertinent to job performance, the types of work experience that you have had, and the duties and responsibilities involved. As you jot down the various items, evaluate your experience and imagine how your experience can contribute to the business career you are seeking. Be careful to be accurate in your descriptions, but place greater emphasis on those items that are more relevant to the jobs for which you are applying. Even if your work experience has been only in low-level jobs, see whether the pattern indicates ambition, drive, eagerness for growth, leadership, management skills, found ability, and ability to get along with others. Make a note of your conclusions.

When you have assembled all this information, you can decide how your material should be arranged within your résumé. See page 175 for a sample résumé developed for nonlegal positions. "Standard" résumés may vary from occupation to occupation. What is acceptable for a law firm may not work for an educational institution. Thus, a law school sample résumé is a less reliable guide for nonlegal than for legal jobs. Remember: If you know what field you want to pursue, try to locate résumés that have been used to find jobs in that field, or carefully read job description posted for these positions, and identify phrases and keywords that point to skills likely to be important to the employer, Then, fashion your résumé to appeal to prospective employers by using the sorts of phrases and keywords that are consistent with the skills that you have to offer.

There is no "correct" résumé formula. You want to provide information about yourself and your qualifications in a manner that will best call attention to the most important points at first glance. Legal employers often prefer one-page résumés for entry-level lawyers, but you may need additional space to develop your qualifications for using your legal education in another field.

Once you are satisfied with the arrangement of information, it is time to get the résumé in final form. Whether you choose a basic word-processing program, graphic design software, or a résumé-building program, keep in mind your own ideas about what you want to say about yourself and how you want your résumé to look. Different fonts allow you to produce a typeset look at home. Many types of business prefer a Web-friendly format that they can enter directly into candidate databases. After reviewing the possibilities, choose the final style and select the content. Remember that you can save a basic version of your résumé and create an infinite number of variants, as necessary.

Consider getting feedback from a career counselor or someone who knows résumés in the area of your interest. A skilled critic and editor can help you avoid making a tactical mistake in this critical document.

Finally, and perhaps most important of all, proofread your résumé for errors. A spelling or typographical error on a résumé can be fatal. Look carefully at usage and appearance, as well as spelling. And remember that proofreading is more than spell checking—as you can sea!

In summary, follow these steps to organize and prepare your résumé for distribution:

◆ Collect facts about yourself in light of your job search plans;
◆ Research the businesses and industries you will be pursuing;
◆ Lay out your information in draft form appropriate to the job search;

- Review the draft;
- Get feedback from someone who knows something;
- Create the final form with a view to appearance as well as content;
- Proofread the document;
- Save in an accessible and modifiable medium; and
- Print and distribute the résumé as necessary.

Taking the time to do it right will pay off for you in the end.

Contacting Employers

Do not assume you will always find some central clearinghouse available through which business organizatons may seek you out. Companies often must depend upon candidates to contact them concerning the qualifications they offer. When there is no organized system for bringing you and the prospective employer together, you will need your own system if you are to conduct an effective search.

In deciding the general areas in which you would like to work, focus your search on those companies likely to have substantial activity in that field. Again, you may wish to limit your search geographically. Or you may wish to limit your search to a particular type of business organization such as banks or chemical companies, or any one of a thousand possibilities. Keep in mind that you can expand or contract your search as your circumstances and the results dictate. Determine your priorities, and take charge of your search rather than letting your search run you.

Once you have established the parameters of your search, the next step is to undertake a research program. This step is of particular importance, for you will be exploring the possibilities to match your needs, interests, and abilities. The goal of your research program is to compile information on the employers whom you wish to seek out.

Fortunately, there are ample resource materials to which you can turn. Do not expect to find a list of prospective employers. An individualized job search also means an individualized research program. The end result will be worth that effort. It will provide the basis for a personalized job search.

One of your first activities will probably be to search the Web for sites that match your search criteria. These sites carry a wealth of information. You can access sites online if you know the Web address (or URL, uniform resource locator), or use a search engine. You should be able to find these resources in any sizable research facility or through your own defined search terms.

The Resources Section of this book contains listings for a number of online resources, but you should employ your research skills using a search engine such as Google or Yahoo to track down additional information that will help you. Given the vast amount of information available on the Web, the greatest limitation to finding information is often lack of imagination. If you are a technologically sophisticated job searcher, the information at your fingertips is significantly greater than what is accessible to a manual researcher.

Both LexisNexis and Westlaw provide access to a variety of non-legal databases. Commercial electronic communication networks and CD-ROM libraries also contain a vast amount of information. Looking for opportunities in nonlegal fields may require you to access databases that are unique or proprietary to those fields.

Even in the electronic age, print materials may still have value. The Resources Section of this book lists a number of directories, books, and lists that you might be able to use. Some of these sources appear in both print and electronic formats, though some do not.

Several print resources deserve special mention. *Standard and Poor's* provides an alphabetical listing of corporations throughout the United States, including the addresses and phone numbers of home offices, corporate status, whether a company is a division or subsidiary, listings of directors and executives, annual revenues, products produced or nature of the business, and standard industrial classifications for company activities. Separate volumes provide alphabetical listings of corporations by their industrial classification, alphabetical listings by state and city, and directories of biographical information on the directors and executives listed.

Another useful volume is the *Guide to American Directories,* edited by Bernard T. Klein. This volume is broken down by subject categories and lists directory titles, publishers' addresses, and prices. What may surprise you is the tremendous number of specialized directories. There is almost certain to be one that pertains to your own interests, no matter how specialized.

Still another valuable reference is the Gale Research Company's *Encyclopedia of Associations.* Most associations can provide you with background information in their field, and you can find valuable information on the pages of their publications and other career material. A general letter of inquiry asking about the availability of materials is all you need to get the ball rolling.

Many of the directories are maintained in law libraries and career center libraries at law schools. Business and professional schools may have print resources not available at the law school, but some institutions may restrict access; for example, the business school may restrict its facilities to business students, excluding even law students from the same university. You may have better luck using the services of your undergraduate or graduate school than your law school's university. Your law school career services professional should know what the policies are.

You may want to consider a subscription to periodic publications in areas that interest you. For example, if you are interested in public accounting, you may want to subscribe to magazines for accountants. You may be able to find more up-to-date and useful information in such publications than you would in formal directories.

At the end of your basic research, you should have the names and addresses of specific prospective employers you are interested in contacting, plus some basic background information on various institutions. You should also have general industry information and details on current problems, collected from business and government publications.

As you develop your prospect list, you may become particularly interested in several specific organizations. In many instances, you can obtain much more complete information directly from organizations themselves, perhaps on their Web sites. Some sites provide very general information about the organization; other sites offer a wealth of in-depth data you can use. Many companies let you browse through recruitment material and even let you apply for jobs online.

Some organizations also produce special recruiting publications that provide information on the organization's activities, the attractions of its particular location, and the functions in which administrative and management personnel are currently employed. Such publications will give you concrete information that will help you determine whether the type of activity in which you are interested is a substantial one within the organization, and they may also suggest new and interesting areas for you to explore. If you cannot find information on a company's Web site, call or write for hard-copy documents, or check with your university's career services office for help in tracking down this information.

Still another source of information about a corporation is the annual stockholders' report. Although this is obviously a publication intended for a wider readership, it can give you a wealth of background information that will be useful from the moment of your initial contact with that company.

One of the goals of your research program should be to create your own list of potential employers. Names and addresses alone, however, are not enough for an effective job search. You need a system for organizing the information you are acquiring.

What kind of information do you need to know? Any and all that may contribute to a productive contact and promote more effective interviewing. Although there is really no limit to the possible data that can be collected, there are a few basic requirements that you will certainly wish to meet.

♦ *Identify the name of the individual within the business organization who will receive your initial contact.* Try to make it the head of the special area in which you are specifically interested, or as Richard Bolles writes in *What Color Is Your Parachute?* the name of the person with the power to hire you. If you are uncertain, use the head of personnel, a graduate of your undergraduate or graduate school, or another lawyer working for the company. If you have been unable to locate this information in one of your directories, call the company headquarters and ask the operator for the name of the person you need to reach. In the latter event, be sure to ask for the spelling of the name and the exact title. Mistakes on these points can be damaging.

♦ *Collect information on the nature of the company's business.* There is a sound reason for this. You are asking the business organization to be interested in your qualifications as they apply to possible employment. It seems reasonable that they should expect you to take the time and trouble to find out about the products or services of their organization.

◆ *As you develop your information, keep asking yourself these questions:*
   1. What are this employer's needs or problems?
   2. How can my skills help solve their problems?
   3. How will hiring me save them money?

A word of caution, however: hiring you may not be the salvation of the company. Establishing this is not your goal at this point. Rather, you are looking for ways in which your employment will be an asset to the organization. For example, how can your legal training enable you to do the job more quickly, more thoroughly, or more profitably for the organization?

This is basic information, and you undoubtedly will wish to flesh it out with further background to assist you at the interview. Add newspaper and magazine clippings, the brochures mentioned previously, and all valuable information that comes your way in the course of your research—anything that will help you familiarize yourself with each organization.

If you can, locate present or past employees of the organization and interview them to hear the insights they have gained through their employment. Keep in mind that you will encounter differences of opinion. These should not cloud your own judgment; just concentrate on the facts you get.

What is the best way to organize the information you have collected? The most practical answer is to use some kind of searchable and sortable database. You can use a spreadsheet (such as Microsoft Excel), a database (such as Microsoft Access), or some other software tool. You can maintain your notes in a word processing file or even on handwritten note cards, but you should try to develop a system as flexible and sophisticated as possible.

Leave yourself room to make notes on dates of contact, individuals spoken to, and your own observations and comments. Your system should make it easy to enter additional information as you develop it. At a minimum, you will want to save the following information:

- Name of employer
- Street address
- Web site address (URL)
- Primary contact name, e-mail address, and telephone number
- Other contacts, e-mail addresses, and telephone numbers
- Job information
- Other notes
- Record of contacts with the company

You may also want to add additional fields of information to reflect your personal interests or critical information, such as law school attended.

Database programs of varying sophistication are available on the market and are accessible to almost anyone who wants to use them. As with résumé preparation and employer research, technology is a tool that can and should be employed whenever possible, to ease the rigors of the job search.

Letters of Application

Even as you are creating your database of employer prospects, you should develop the general pattern for your letter of application, or cover letter. The résumé itself is a somewhat formal document. The cover letter is your sales pitch. It need be only three paragraphs long.

- In the first paragraph, tell the individual to whom you are writing why you are interested in *this* organization. Look at your research notes for clues. If you have been referred to the employer by a specific contact, this is the place to mention that person by name. Is it the type of activity that has particular appeal? Did the stockholders' report indicate a dynamic and aggressive management team? Is it because of the growth potential of the company? The particular reason you use is not important; you want to show that you are interested enough in that particular organization to find out something about it. Your geographic preferences, for example, are probably not pertinent. You want to feature something about the company that made you want to contact them.

- ◆ The second paragraph should refer to your résumé and your particular qualifications for the opportunity you are seeking. Be clear that you are applying for a nonlegal position and focus on the skills of your legal education that relate to effective job performance. This paragraph should pique the reader's interest sufficiently to motivate him or her to turn the page and look at your résumé.

- ◆ The third paragraph should specifically state the objective of your communication. "I am interested in arranging an interview for employment with your company" may seem too direct, but it clearly states the purpose of your contact and is therefore more likely to produce action. Many cover letters leave this important question open, which tends to be a mistake. The final sentence of this last paragraph should include a street address, e-mail address, or phone number where you can be reached. Do not worry that this information also appears on your résumé. On the résumé, its purpose is to provide information; in the cover letter, it is to inspire action. Remember to make sure that the answer message on your voice mail is professional in nature during the period of your job search.

Because cover letters must be individually written, addressed to a specific person, and tailored to each organization (giving your reasons for contact), producing the letters may seem like an insurmountable task if you do not have some kind of mail-merge capability. Microsoft Word and other word processing programs enable you to create personalized applications. If you keep the raw data in a database or spreadsheet, you will need to download your files into a word processing format. Keep in mind, however, that all your applications do not have to be done at once. They can be done in small batches, as you do more research and develop new contacts. It may help to divide the project into manageable segments, such as five or ten letters per week.

Although technology allows you to generate more letters than you could write manually, it is still critical to personalize the letters and send out only a manageable number at a given time. Because just about everyone has access to word processors today, the value of generic cover letters is diminishing through overuse.

Many companies today permit online applications. Check the Web site to determine whether this is the case. If it is, use the online process. It may be more difficult to personalize an online form, but do your best.

A final note: if you have a personal entrée to an organization, nothing beats face-to-face communication, so pick up the phone and call for an appointment. If you have an inside contact, an informal meeting for lunch or drinks may be the best first step. Use discretion and do not presume familiarity that is not there, but if you know someone on the inside, go straight for your contact.

Interviewing

Because the human resources office may be a major stumbling block for legally trained persons seeking business careers, because of lack of understanding of how legal skills can translate into the business environment, let us consider how you can leverage the human resources professionals you encounter. Probably the easiest way is to put yourself in the other person's shoes.

The people you contact in an HR department measure their job performance by their ability to recruit and hire the most-qualified employees to fill company needs. Unlike in many law firms, your résumé will be read by someone who is experienced in gleaning the important information efficiently and rapidly. Thus, it is in the human resource administrator's best interest, as well as yours, to communicate as freely and fully as possible. This type of approach gives you and the company representative a common goal: to find a position that uses your talents to the fullest and thereby offers the best possibility for advancement. Human resources professionals, because of their experience, can be strong allies in your search for the right position—but only if you let them. The better the relationship you develop with the HR professional, the better your chances of opening the right doors in an organization.

If the organization is small and does not have a human resources department, or if you are able to make direct contact with department managers, your initial interview may be with a manager in the area of interest you have indicated.

Before an interview, refresh your memory by reviewing your file on the organization. In addition, take time to sit down with your résumé and review it in light of the kind of questions you may be asked. If you have publications or writing samples, take some time to review them, so that you can talk about them intelligently. Think about the most important and positive things you want to say about yourself.

You are likely to find that the skilled nonlegal employment interviewer conducts the interview quite differently from the law office employer, who may engage in the interviewing process only periodically. In part, the difference in approach reflects the different goals of the interviewers. The law office interviewer seeks to determine what kind of a lawyer you will make, whereas the business interviewer seeks to determine not only the skills you bring to the job, but also your potential for advancement within the organization.

Because the approach is likely to be different, you should think about the types of questions you are probably going to be asked. You may be surprised at the range of questions in the interview. The interviewer is seeking, within the relatively short space of the interview, to get to know you as a person. There is a limited amount of time in which to obtain as much information as possible.

Of course, you can expect questions concerning your educational background, but not just about your legal training. Do not be surprised if the interviewer asks you which subjects you liked best in elementary school, or, conversely, which you liked least. Anticipate being asked about your work experience, including what you did best and where you felt you were less effective. Questions about how you felt about teachers and supervisors are almost routine. Do not be surprised if you are asked to describe your formative years or the differences you see between yourself and your siblings. Obviously, such questions are somewhat difficult to respond to off the cuff, so by thinking of them before the interview, you will be better prepared to respond.

The interview is not an inquisition. Rather, the aim of the interviewer is to discover your reaction to the people and activities you have encountered in your life. The facts about you are in your résumé and in the application form you probably completed before the interview. The interviewer is seeking information about the kind of person you are, how you relate to others, and what special strengths you feel you have. Even the best résumé and application cannot supply that.

In fact, the more skilled the interviewer, the more you will find that you enjoy the interview. It will be a conversation—a conversation about you—and who does not enjoy that? With a skilled interviewer, however, there is no doubt about who is in charge of the interview.

Another aim of the interviewer is to learn what skills you have that would enhance your job performance. This obviously gives you the opportunity to discuss how your legal education is applicable. In addition, the analysis you did in preparing to write your résumé is most useful. Think of the skills applicable to the position for which you are applying and of the flexibility that will help you meet the future requirements of advanced positions with greater responsibilities. Whenever you interview, try to communicate these skills clearly and persuasively to the interviewer.

Keep in mind your intangible skills as well your tangible ones. For example, how do you perform as a leader? How do you deal with problems? How do your peers react to you? How do you deal with difficult people? Answers to these questions will help you highlight skills of which you may not have been aware.

A single interview within a business organization is unlikely to result in an employment offer. If the initial interview is with someone in the personnel department, no decision will be reached until you have talked with one or more people who would be supervising you. Their questions may be different, but the essential approach will be the same.

You will have your most effective interview if you relax. None of us appears at our best when we are nervous or tense, yet most people find it difficult to relax under the tensions of an interview. In general, the more you know about the organization, and the better ᴀve analyzed your abilities, interests, and future plans, the easiᴇr the interview process becomes for you. But you can take specific steps like deep breathing or relaxation techniques before the interview if you feel the pressure becoming unmanageable.

All of us have experienced meeting someone where the chemistry just was not there. Remember how you struggled to establish rapport without any information to get the conversation rolling? It may help to have some kind of icebreaker ready to start the conversation if the interviewer is not. The problem may not be lack of chemistry, but simply the awkwardness of a stressful moment, so be ready to keep the flow of the conversation going at all times. In business terms, your most successful employment interviews are those in which you can speak conversationally with the interviewer. A good interviewer will create a positive atmosphere, but be ready to initiate interesting discussion if the interviewer does not.

As a lawyer interviewing for nonlegal employment, there are five questions you may be asked that can be characterized as hurdles. For each of these questions, as with any difficult question that you anticipate facing, it helps to develop a good answer in advance. This eliminates the need to come up with an explanation on the spot and conveys the impression that you are either thoughtful, quick on your feet, or both. Addressing these issues in advance also forces you to take stock of yourself, because, if you cannot satisfy yourself with your answer, you are not likely to satisfy a prospective employer:

- Why don't you want to practice law?
- Why shouldn't I hire someone who is trained in this field?
- What if I can't pay you what you are worth based on your legal experience?
- How do I know that you won't leave and go back to the practice of law?
- Don't lawyers just get in the way of solving problem in an organization?

Certainly, there are no easy answers to these questions, and anyone who tells you otherwise is either naive or dishonest. With some thought, you should be able to come up with good answers that are neither simplistic nor convoluted and rambling. In a sense, these questions should be viewed as invitations for you to sell yourself.

If the interviewer challenges you with questions like these, he is in a sense asking you to refute the underlying presumption that you are not qualified for the job; this may give you a chance to reinforce your reasons for pursuing this nonlegal position. If this happens, think of yourself as arguing a case for a client, and the client is you. As a lawyer, your job is to develop persuasive arguments, and this is no different. The interviewer is picking at the weaknesses in your case. To the extent that you prepare for and answer such questions, you improve your chances of meeting your burden of persuasion.

Although law students and young lawyers do not often think of oral advocacy as a tool in the interviewing process, clearly it is. Furthermore, it is a tool whose value is enhanced outside of the employment market for traditional legal jobs. When you interview for legal jobs, everyone has legal training and is on relatively equal footing when it comes to skills of oral advocacy. When you step into the nonlegal job market, you are likely to be in a distinct minority, and your skill as an advocate becomes a proportionately greater asset.

Remember that persuasiveness is context based, so keep your audience in mind. Listen actively to what the interviewer has to say and frame your statements in a way your listener will understand. The point is that your legal training has provided you with the tools to be persuasive—use them wisely.

Procrastination

Procrastination is the archenemy of every job search program. As early as you possibly can in your law school career, you should begin developing your research program, your résumé, and your cover letter. You should practice your interviewing skills whenever possible. If you have graduated from law school already and find yourself thinking about career alternatives, now is the perfect time to get serious about pursuing your options.

Do not worry if this seems too far in advance of your availability for full-time employment. Large organizations (like large law firms) plan their recruiting for management trainee spots well in advance of the development of specific openings. They know it will take a great deal of time to identify the persons they wish to employ. Of course, it will also take you considerable time to complete your total job search program. Once your well-planned program is underway, requests for interviews are certain to develop.

You may be somewhat discouraged when you contemplate the amount of research required, the difficult self-analysis necessary to produce a good résumé, and the multitude of contacts and interviews you face. Keep in mind, however, that an effective job search has as its aim a challenging and interesting position, in which you can contribute to the organization all the skills and abilities you possess. Only rarely is it a one-shot deal.

Because there is no end-of-term grade or regular paycheck coming in to test how well your job search program is going, plan to reward yourself for maximum performance at each step along the way. This reward need not be expensive. For example, it could be an hour of reading just for pleasure. Whatever you choose, all that is necessary is to remind yourself that you are giving this important endeavor your best effort. A reward provides a tremendous boost to your own morale, a big advantage in any job search.

Creating a Business

Some of those who enter nonlegal careers do not go to work for a company or any other kind of ongoing organization. They create their own business. These are the entrepreneurs—individuals who see an opportunity in the marketplace and take advantage of it.

When you go to work for an organization, you are selling all of your time to that organization. When you go to work as a principal in a law practice, you are selling your time to clients on the open market. When you open a business, you are selling your talents to yourself for the purposes of the entrepreneurial venture.

If you decide to go into business for yourself, remember that it takes a special kind of person to succeed: someone very sure of herself; someone willing to take risks; someone who can weather a slow period of startup and forego short-term rewards in favor of long-term satisfaction; someone who is comfortable and skillful at selling herself in the marketplace. With the caveat that starting a business is not for everyone, however, it is a path that many lawyers have taken. If you are contemplating a nonlegal career, you should at least consider the possibility of opening your own business at the same time you are thinking about going to work for someone else.

When starting a business, instead of writing a cover letter and résumé, you prepare a business plan. Instead of selling yourself to an interviewer, you sell your plan to a banker, potential partners, or investors. Instead of proving yourself to supervisors on your job, you market yourself to purchasers of your services. Instead of managing your own work, you manage an entire business. This is the same challenge faced by lawyers who practice alone or in very small firms. See *The Lawyer's Guide to Creating a Business Plan: A Step-by-Step Software Package,* by Linda Pinson (ABA, 2006) for additional information on creating a business plan.

Whether inside or outside of the practice of law, the question comes down to whether you want to work for yourself or somebody else, and whether you want the guarantee of a salary or the risk of a return on your investment in time and capital. See Chapter 14 for more information on entrepreneurial activities by lawyers in nonlegal careers.

Summary

Numerous opportunities are available for lawyers who no longer desire a traditional law practice. A law degree can open doors to career opportunities in any work setting. Imagination is all you need to find a potential career in a nonlegal setting.

Many possibilities are discussed in the next four chapters, but the opportunities described there are by no means exhaustive. They are meant to stimulate your imagination and inspire you to further investigate any field in which your interest is piqued.

Some of the positions will be more "legal" than others. Some of the positions will require daily use of legal skills in nontraditional settings, whereas others will not require any knowledge or understanding of the law. In these situations, your law degree simply provides you with additional education that sets you apart from your peers in the industry.

Career Opportunities in the Nonlegal Sector

Careers in Business and Industry 7

Lawyers can be found at all levels, in every type of work situation in business. Although the traditional setting for a lawyer in business has been the general counsel's office, lawyers seeking more-diverse opportunities have moved into management. Many of the new lawyers who have targeted an industry have taken entry-level positions in that industry, bypassing the general counsel's office. The additional education is a credential that sets lawyers apart from others in the industry and often facilitates rapid advancement.

There are now more lawyers in administrative and management positions than there are in corporate legal departments. Business acumen is a prized skill, but some companies view the law degree as a valuable tool to enhance job performance. These companies have been willing to pay for part-time law study while an employee continues on the job.

At a certain level of management in every company, business experience becomes more important to the position than legal training. Although there are many lawyers in the top positions at some of the largest corporations in the world, the people in those positions are usually business people rather than lawyers. Although their legal training may have helped them rise to the top, it is their business acumen that allows them to maintain the position.

Corporations and Their Departments

The diversity of corporate positions currently held by people with legal training is evidence of the vast range of opportunity open to anyone who decides that a career in business is more compatible with their interests and abilities than traditional practice.

Entry-level positions for employees with legal training vary radically from industry to industry. Although you might expect your legal training to land you a management position the minute you walk in the door, remember that your education has not trained you to be an expert in management, marketing, personnel, or the workings of a specific industry. People with MBAs have a distinct advantage in the entry-level business position.

In some industries, management trainees start in the mailroom. Most companies, however, do not require that rite-of-subservient-passage. Many management trainee programs do require employees to work in the field to experience the various jobs within the corporation. This practical experience helps managers understand the problems created by policy decisions.

Because of the diversity of corporate structures, the various jobs described in this chapter are grouped by function rather than by specific titles. For example, some corporations consider the tax department to be a part of the legal department, whereas others assign the tax function to the financial operations department. By using the function approach in your job search, you will not be foreclosed from finding information on potential positions simply because the particular department designation used by the organization does not match the one you specify.

Tax Department

Considering the total activity of a corporate tax department, it is not difficult to understand the perennial debate as to whether tax is a financial or legal function. It is both. At the entry level, the work involves collecting the corporation's financial performance information and preparing the more than five hundred tax forms that must be filed to meet federal, state, and local tax reporting requirements. Reports are prepared to substantiate the tax returns. Some of the various reports include income tax, sales tax, use tax, property tax, franchise tax, payroll tax, and license fees. Background reports must be prepared to substantiate the tax filings and reports to stockholders. At the entry-level positions, the tax function is financial.

Senior members of the tax department are involved in more diverse tasks. These tasks include:

- Supervising the review of tax returns—This involves the review of tax returns of domestic affiliates and foreign affiliates, if the company has any. It also includes supervising the conduct of federal, state, and local (and possibly foreign) tax audits and examinations. Part of the audit supervision function includes developing amicable professional relationships with the tax auditors from the various governmental and regulatory agencies.
- Supervising tax litigation—This function includes supervising and reviewing the preparation and argument of protests of administrative actions and claims for refunds. This may include participating in court litigation, either directly or through the supervision of outside counsel.
- Advising management about taxes—This includes advising management about the tax effects of transactions and suggesting alternate ways to structure the deal. Frequently this type of work involves property acquisition or the purchase or sale of business subsidiaries.
- Tax lobbying—This function involves seeking lawfully to influence proposed tax legislation and regulations by meeting with members of the congressional tax-writing committees and their staffs, as well as with members of the government relations department. These activities may be undertaken individually or through a trade association or professional group. Similar lobbying activities are required at the state and local levels.

- Advising on foreign tax issues—This includes advising the international divisions of a multinational corporation regarding taxes of foreign countries and the related effects of foreign operations on United States taxes, to determine proper planning and compliance.
- Financial planning—This function involves initiating tax advice as part of the corporation's financial planning process.
- Seminars—This includes conducting seminars, meetings, and continuing education programs for appropriate corporate personnel, to inform them of relevant developments in the tax field that affect their operations.

These tax department positions combine the law with accounting to produce a businessperson with the background to move to the highest positions within the corporation. Because of the complex nature of corporate tax compliance, some corporations require that all of the senior managers have some legal training. Most corporations consider legal training as desirable but not required. An accounting undergraduate degree is mandatory unless it is replaced by a graduate degree in business tax or accounting.

▼▼▼▼▼

John was an accountant before entering law school. He had passed the CPA exam right before law school began. After law school and the bar, he took a position in the audit department of a Big Five accounting firm. John enjoyed working for the accounting firm and working with the people in the financial departments of some of the largest corporations in the world. After five years at the accounting firm, John was encouraged to apply for a position with one of the firms he had been working with as an auditor. The chief financial officer liked John and offered him a position as a vice president of finance. John took the position so that he could improve his pay, hours, and benefits. He also took the job so that he could work his way into a chief financial officer position at his new company, or at a different one, after a few more years of work. Although John's CPA credential got him in the door, his law degree helped him understand and write the financial reports that made him an invaluable asset to his company.

There are several business schools that offer a master's degree in business taxation (MBT) in conjunction with their J.D. programs. An LL.M. degree in tax can also substitute for the undergraduate accounting degree. Passing the CPA examination may be required for several high-level positions within the tax department. Interestingly, the CPA exam includes a section on law.

▼▼▼▼▼

Juanita went to work for the Internal Revenue Service immediately following law school. She signed a four-year contract with the IRS so that the government would pay for her to get an LL.M. from Georgetown University. Juanita worked for the IRS and attended school at night. After the four years with the IRS, she contacted her university career services office to find out about corporate in-house positions. She sent her résumé to several companies and took a job with a major corporation in the tax department at their headquarters office. Juanita could have made more money by taking a job with a large law firm, but she chose the corporate position so that she could enjoy a better life balance.

Human Resources or the Employee Relations Department

Depending on the corporation, this function may also be called industrial relations, labor relations, human resources, or personnel administration. Included within this department are several distinct functions, which will be discussed separately. The desirability of having law school-trained personnel employed in these activities is evident in the substantial number of lawyers now occupying these positions.

Most companies appear to apply the term *labor relations* to the activities surrounding the development and implementation of the company's labor policies and procedures, including its relationship with unions. Individuals working in this area may be involved in one or more of these activities. Work may include negotiation of the various corporate labor agreements within previously approved economic limits, as well as monitoring labor relations matters throughout the corporation to ensure adherence to applicable labor agreements and corporate labor-relations policies.

In some cases, employees in this field develop and present the company's position in arbitration cases, or handle National Labor Relations Board (NLRB) unfair labor practice charges and representation situations. On a continuing basis, they review labor-relations policies and practices as well as labor agreements to ensure compliance with applicable federal and state laws.

People in this field find it imperative to keep current on proposed labor legislation, NLRB decisions, court decisions, and Equal Employment Opportunity Commission (EEOC) rulings, including safety, security, and fair employment practices. They need to determine what effect, if any, these developments have on continuing corporate labor agreements, practices, policies, and procedures, and to inform the affected supervisors. On occasion, they participate in the settlement of labor disputes, arbitrations, grievances, and other employee and union relations matters.

The term *labor relations* implies a rapport between management and labor. A person in this position who maintains an amicable and fair relationship with union leadership and workers between contract negotiations can expect less acrimony during the contract-negotiation process. By working with other industry representatives, either directly or through trade associations, harmonious employee relations may be achieved through maintenance of equitable and competitive wage policies.

Employee benefits is an area where legal training can be a tremendous benefit to the individual and to the corporation. As the cost of benefits rises and the complexity of the various plans increases to control costs, legal training allows the benefits manager to negotiate fair plans and avoid contractual loopholes that may cost the company millions of dollars in future claims. This area may involve planning, developing, implementing, and administering a variety of benefit programs, including (but not limited to) medical and dental insurance, long-term disability, and retirement benefits. The funding and administration of the benefit plan may be handled by the department rather than by an outside vendor, depending on the size of the corporation and the complexity of the plan. An integral part of any employee benefit program is communicating about the program with the employees involved.

Many corporations have an individual who deals strictly with the company's implementation of the equal employment opportunities program. This involves developing internal policies to ensure compliance with EEOC legislation, analyzing current company practices, and recommending courses of action. Although this function is now separate from the labor-relations function in many corporations, it must be closely coordinated within the labor relations area to foster a harmonious workplace.

In addition to the above areas where legal training is becoming an essential credential for the position, employees who have legal training also work in the administration of workers' compensation programs, in the recruitment and training of employees, and in wage and salary administration. These jobs have traditionally been held by people without legal training, but a law degree should give an applicant an edge as an additional academic credential.

▼▼▼▼▼

Samantha was a manager in the labor relations department of her corporation when she decided to go to law school. With the blessing of her company, she enrolled in a local law school's part-time night program. Samantha's company agreed to pay her tuition as long as she agreed to continue to work for the company for four years after her graduation from law school. She worked full time during the day at her management job and attended school at night. Samantha had a difficult time juggling work and school, but she graduated and passed the bar. Following graduation, Samantha was promoted to vice president in the labor relations department. She received a substantial raise with the promotion. Immediately following her promotion, headhunters started calling her with new opportunities. Samantha told them that she needed to stay with her company for four years or she would have to pay back her company for her law school tuition. One headhunter told her that the new company would be willing to buy her out of her four-year commitment by paying the tuition she would owe, plus a bonus and raise. Samantha has resisted the temptation to leave, so far, because she likes her company and her coworkers. Samantha's law degree has paid dividends and raised her stock inside and outside the company.

▼▼▼▼▼

Don was an associate in a medium-size labor law firm. During his second year at the firm, he was assigned to assist a senior partner with an important trial for a large union. Don worked closely with the senior partner and the executive director of the union (also a lawyer) during the pretrial preparation phase. Once the trial began, Don sat second chair to the senior partner who handled the trial. The executive director liked Don's work ethic and insights and, following the trial, offered Don a job with the union. After five years at the union, Don became executive director when his mentor retired.

Finance Department

No corporation functions without a financial control center. Depending on the corporation, this department is known as the treasurer's office, comptroller's office, or the accounting and finance department. Some corporations also include a separate and distinct internal audit department, which on a day-to-day basis performs duties similar to those of an outside auditor, but in greater depth.

The functions of the financial office vary according to the nature of the corporation's business activities. At a minimum, the activities include the establishment and maintenance of company-wide accounting and financial reporting policies and practices. If there is an internal audit department, the financial office works with it to assure compliance.

The financial office develops and maintains a financial reporting and analysis system, which permits management to develop both short-range and long-range plans. In addition, financial statements and reports must be prepared for investors, lenders, the Securities and Exchange Commission (SEC), the board of directors, financial analysts, and investment bankers. Forecasting the potential effect on the company's financial status of proposed equity changes, regulatory actions, changes in world financial conditions, and changes in accounting practices is another function of the financial department.

Custody and protection of funds, securities, and other financial instruments, as well as banking, the receipt of funds, and the disbursement of funds are additional functions of the financial department. The office evaluates the need for procurement of funds and the investment of surplus. In some instances, the financial office is also responsible for customer credit arrangements and the negotiation of term-loan agreements. Budget preparation, monitoring, and financial forecasting are also major responsibilities.

An undergraduate degree in finance or economics is an important credential for success in a corporate finance department. A tax background may be substituted if supplemented with courses in managerial economics and corporate finance. Because this department sets financial policies for the company, an MBA degree, MBT degree, CPA credential, or an LL.M. degree in banking or tax can provide the academic background for a rapid rise to the top of the department. Many corporate presidents, chief executive officers, and chief operations officers come from the finance department. A legal background broadens a businessperson's understanding of the ramifications of implementation of capital plans.

Opportunities in the financial area are not confined to industry. Opportunities for lawyers with an interest in finance are also found in banks and financial institutions, investment houses, and brokerage firms. Banks and brokerage firms are covered below.

Government and Public Affairs Departments

Many areas of corporate activity involve meeting the requirements of various laws and regulations issued by governmental agencies and departments. In the government relations area, the industry seeks to bring its influence to bear upon pending legislation. A corporation may do this in a series of steps.

The first step is a continuing analysis of all pending federal, state, and local legislation for its possible impact on the company's operations. If it is determined that particular legislation under consideration relates to the company's interests, the second step is to define the company's position on the issue. This determination is made in consultation with the officers of the company, interested internal departments, and often with trade association boards and committees. The position taken may be for or against the proposed legislation, or it may recommend changes or amendments. The third step involves presenting the company's position to the appropriate governmental officials. This lobbying may take the form of formal written statements, testimony before legislative bodies, or informal, personal discussions. The latter meetings are facilitated by maintaining a cordial relationship with government officials who are most likely to be concerned with the matters under consideration. Development of these relationships is a major responsibility of government-relations personnel. They also may cooperate with other departments having direct relationships with specific agencies—for example, the employee-relations group with its relationship with the EEOC.

When pending legislation is of industry-wide concern, the company's lobbying may be coordinated through professional or trade associations. In fact, trade associations also offer employment opportunities for those interested in government relations. They frequently represent companies that are not large enough to maintain an internal government relations staff.

Consumer Affairs and Public Relations Departments

Although markedly different in function, consumer affairs and public relations have one thing in common with government affairs—a positive outreach and impact by the company on the public and consumers.

Public relations and government activities are often intertwined, because both involve the image of the organization and contacts with the media. In many companies these functions are combined in one department. Public relations, unlike government relations, deals specifically with public perceptions and consumer attitudes toward the company, its products, and services.

From time to time, matters may develop that go beyond specific company or industry concerns and the need arises to develop public opinion. In addition to coordinating the activities of various company departments that are involved with the issue, there may also be efforts to coordinate with the work being done by other companies in the industry, consumer groups, and others who have an interest in the matter.

In the consumer affairs area, individuals work to assure that consumer complaints and information requests are handled promptly and fairly. Accurate and useful product information, including warranty information, is prepared by this group. In addition, consumer affairs persons may also provide guidance and advice on product safety. The public affairs department seeks to create a positive image; occasionally it may need to counteract bad publicity. The department works with a broad segment of the company's divisions, and this may include contact with vendors. Close coordination with the legal department is essential in handling inquiries from concerned organizations and governmental agencies. The information must be formulated and delivered in a manner that assures the interested party that the company has a thorough understanding of the legal impact of government policy affecting product safety and consumer affairs.

The environmental concerns of some companies, aside from regulatory compliance, have led to the development of activities that communicate the company's position to concerned individuals and organizations. In general, the activities in this area are similar to those pursued in consumer affairs and product safety. All of these activities may be grouped under a single designation such as public relations or public affairs. In other companies, the public relations function will primarily relate to providing information to the business community and those individuals interested in the company's business, its products, its officers, its plans, and its programs.

Creating and projecting a company's image and position in response to the broad interests and concerns of the public and government is a day-to-day concern of business organizations and involves a significant number of people. Minimum requirements include a background in public relations, governmental compliance, or marketing. Legal training is a definite asset for any job requiring a government liaison. More and more lawyers are finding that their legal skills can make a substantial contribution to these efforts.

▼▼▼▼▼

Joseph made the decision to go to law school because he wanted to run for public office. He did not want to practice law, but he would if it would help him reach his goal. Joseph worked in a law firm during the summer following his second year in law school and realized that he did not want to have to practice law to realize his goal. During his third year in law school, he contacted the legislator for whom he had been a campaign worker. Joseph asked for a job as a legislative aide and was hired following graduation. Joseph moved to Washington, D.C., and decided not to take the bar exam. Joseph worked his way up in the legislator's office and ultimately replaced the chief legislative analyst. After working in Washington for a couple of years, his boss encouraged Joseph to apply for a position as a White House Fellow. Following his year as a White House Fellow working in the Department of Education, Joseph took a position with a prominent lobbying firm in Washington. He has not totally abandoned the idea of returning home and running for office someday, but right now he enjoys the access he has to members of Congress and the White House, and is very happy working as a lobbyist.

Transportation Department

The type of activities that fall under the heading of transportation (referred to as traffic in some companies) varies considerably, depending on the nature of the corporation. If a company's activities involve the movement of raw materials to production areas and finished products to consumers, warehouses, and other storage locations, then plans and procedures for their transportation must be formulated and monitored. In some cases, this process involves the ownership or leasing of private carriers.

If you have never worked in a corporation, it is highly unlikely that you have considered transportation activities as an area in which your legal training could be an advantage. Because of the diversity of the work, there are a number of lawyers involved in the transportation departments in major corporations.

Employees involved in this area must analyze transportation facilities and commodity classifications to determine the most efficient and economical shipping rates and routes and must furnish this data to other departments and customers. Investigations of damages during shipment, delays, overcharges, and insurance charges must be initiated. In some instances, the duties of transportation managers include studies in product planning, warehousing, packaging, and loading to reduce shipping costs.

This area may involve planning for and purchasing transportation equipment, or leasing equipment and warehouse facilities from other entities. It may include appearing before federal and state agencies on tariffs and similar matters of interest to private carriers. The globalization of trade increasingly involves the transportation department in the application of treaties and of international and foreign law.

Employees working in transportation with companies that move people, as well as freight, by air, motor, rail, or water have additional responsibilities. They must formulate and determine freight or passenger classifications and applicable rates according to company policies and governmental regulations. These employees are constantly evaluating existing rate structures to determine their economic suitability and evaluating the schedules to determine adequacy of service.

New rate tables and schedules may be developed to meet the company's changing economic needs, expansion or line abandonment plans, or both. An understanding of the economic and legal issues involved in developing a competitive tariff is essential for an individual in this position.

The department negotiates contracts with other companies for the transportation of freight or passengers in areas not served by the company, including the determination of the division of interline revenue. Supervision of or coordination with receiving and shipping departments, reservation and ticket offices, and those engaged in soliciting freight or passenger business are also important functions.

The transportation department may negotiate the leasing of satellite time to transmit radio and television programs to the individual stations of a network, and arrange for facilities to transmit programs from the point of broadcast origin to network stations.

Because lawyers outside of corporate activity are often unaware of the existence of these functions that are necessary to so many corporations, relatively few lawyers are presently working in the area. By its nature, however, it is an area in which legal training proves advantageous to job performance. The work involves extensive collection of data, analysis of facts, recommendation for action, negotiation, and work with regulatory agencies. Legal training should give you an edge in applying for a transportation job.

▼▼▼▼▼

Ann went to work at a law firm immediately after graduating from law school. She was content with the work, but the long hours were wearing on her. When a position as an in-house lawyer opened up in a corporation that she had worked with on behalf of the firm, she seized the opportunity. While working in-house, Ann was assigned to work with the transportation department. When the head of the department retired, Ann asked for the position and got it. She received a raise and the title of vice president. Ann says that she would never have known that such a position existed had she not worked for the company first. She loves her new position, where she gets to combine her business acumen with her legal experience.

Risk Management

It would be difficult to imagine any corporation or business organization without an insurance program, or risk management, as it is sometimes known. The only difference between the two is what is dictated by the varying needs of the organization and the number of persons necessary to accomplish the individual company's objectives. Several distinct activities are involved:

◆ Risk management involves analysis of all corporate risks of accidental occurrences, both actual and potential, in the areas of property loss, loss of income, workers' compensation, and liability. Determining such risks may involve surveys of company property, assets, and operations to classify hazards and evaluate insurable risks. Consultation with engineering, human resources, and financial departments may be necessary to plan insurance risk coverage, as well as negotiation with insurance brokers to purchase adequate coverage at the lowest possible cost.

◆ It is necessary for a person working in this area to keep up with insurance industry developments such as new areas of coverage, as well as current insurance legislation, so that risk coverage may be changed or modified as needed.

◆ The risk management unit prepares records and reports on experience-cost-analysis, and safety and loss-prevention summaries, for the guidance of management.

◆ Negotiation of the settlement of loss claims with insurance carriers and cooperation with the legal department to provide information for the litigation of insured risks are among the responsibilities in this area. In addition, all insurance contracts must be audited to determine whether any changes in insurance requirements and coverage are needed.

Within the insurance industry itself, lawyers work in almost every aspect of a company's activities. These include most of the common areas of concern to all corporate entities, as well as the development or revision of specific insurance programs to meet anticipated demand. Thus, one of the functions of in-house risk management is to manage outside legal costs. Who would be better positioned to manage outside lawyers than an inside lawyer?

In addition to in-house risk management, many lawyers work for insurance companies in a variety of capacities. Areas of insurance company activity comparable to those found in other industries need not be reiterated. Entry into these positions will, in most cases, be comparable to that in other industries. See the "Insurance Companies" section below.

Health care has become a runaway expense for firms offering health care benefits to their employees. Health insurance costs have caused companies to reevaluate the type and scope of coverage they can offer their employees. Cost containment through reduced benefits, higher deductibles, higher employee contributions, and fewer provider choices forces employers to make difficult decisions. As health care costs rise, experts in risk management, contract administration, and human resources are needed to design company programs that meet the needs of the employees while remaining affordable.

Companies with union employees have special challenges in their attempts to control health care benefits. Skillful negotiators craft the compromises required of both the companies and employees that are necessary to maintain satisfactory benefits at economical levels.

In the future, political solutions may simplify the process. Until this occurs, the health insurance area needs educated and talented administrators. Many companies devote a substantial part of their government-relations efforts to health care reform.

▼▼▼▼▼

Kendra was having a difficult time finding a job for the summer following her second year of law school because she really didn't know what she wanted to do. When she saw a job posted at the career planning office for a small insurance defense firm, she applied. All summer she worked on preparing to defend insurance companies in court. Her supervising partner took her to court to observe one of the trials toward the end of the summer. After her summer experience, Kendra still wasn't sure what she wanted to do. She didn't think she wanted to be a litigator, even though she enjoyed her summer at the firm. In the fall of her third year, she saw a job posting for in-house positions at the headquarters of a major insurance company. She signed up for an interview and was offered the job based on her previous experience with the insurance defense firm. Kendra joined the company shortly after finishing the bar exam. The company started Kendra as a claims adjuster so that she could learn the business. Following her training, Kendra moved into the legal department where she worked on settling major accident claims. After two years working in the legal department, she heard that her alma mater was looking for a director of risk management. She applied for the job and was hired. Kendra was able to negotiate a comparable salary so she did not have to sacrifice to work for her alma mater. She enjoys being on campus and helping her college.

Regulatory Compliance Department

Because of the proliferation of government regulatory activity at all levels—federal, state, and local—hardly a business or industry remains untouched by the need to assure compliance with the various rules and regulations. Often the economic well-being of the company is at stake.

Because of the complexities involved in assuring compliance and the importance of this function to the economic aspects of a company, it is not surprising to find more and more lawyers gravitating to this area. In some companies compliance is handled directly by the operating unit affected by the regulation, such as equal employment opportunity being assigned to the employee-relations department. In other companies, by contrast, all regulatory compliance matters are supervised from a central unit.

It is impossible to list here all of the types of activities that may be carried out under the general designation of regulatory compliance. A partial listing of the functions performed in a single company involved in the production of drugs, cosmetics, and devices in meeting the requirements of the Food and Drug Administration (FDA), the U.S. Department of Agriculture (USDA), and the Federal Trade Commission (FTC), however, will give you some idea of the nature of the work:

- ◆ Coordinate and supervise all activities involved in the preparation of technical data for submission to government agencies such as the FDA, USDA, and FTC.
- ◆ Gather, organize, prepare, assemble, and submit information for investigational new drug submissions and new drug applications in accordance with new drug regulations, reviewing them for completeness and accuracy.
- ◆ Negotiate with the FDA with regard to product claims, and coordinate contacts for the company with FDA scientific-review personnel.
- ◆ Serve as the company representative during plant inspections by FDA personnel.
- ◆ Coordinate training sessions for manufacturing and control personnel under simulated FDA inspection conditions.

- Review and approve labeling, advertising, and specifications to assure compliance with FDA regulations.
- Coordinate preparations and submit periodic reports, including literature surveys, required by government agencies when marketing new drugs.
- Assemble and summarize data in response to specific trade association or government agency requests for data.
- Serve as liaison in coordinating activities between the company and government agencies by acquiring information on new guidelines, regulations, and amendments.
- Summarize regulatory information to be supplied to other operating units and companies.

Working in any of the above areas requires a technical background, even though legal training would provide substantial assistance in determining the requirements to be met. Not all regulatory compliance areas require a technical understanding of the products. Nevertheless, familiarity with the operation of the functions being regulated is essential in monitoring compliance. For example, someone working in a publicly held company is required to file regular reports with various state and federal agencies, depending on the nature of the business and the level of regulation exerted by the governmental entity.

Another area of activity is collecting, reading, analyzing, summarizing, and commenting on written government regulations, and training others to comply with them. Legal training is useful and frequently employed in the formulation of plans and procedures for compliance. Lawyers are trained to understand regulations and to determine whether contemplated procedures will accomplish necessary results.

Corporate Secretarial Department

Long before people with law degrees were working in the regulatory compliance area, lawyers were involved in the corporate secretarial area. Indeed, it is not uncommon for the title *secretary* to also be held by the general counsel. Thus, this area was one of the first to demonstrate that nonlegal positions within a corporation could benefit from the attention of legally trained minds.

The corporate secretarial office is responsible for keeping the minutes of shareholder meetings, board meetings, and sometimes executive committee meetings. The corporate secretary maintains records of specific information on shareholders, notifies shareholders of meetings, and furnishes proxy ballots when required and in accordance with SEC rules. An important function is the preparation of proxy statements.

The secretary is responsible for the corporate seal and for having it affixed to documents as directed by the board of directors. The board may also direct the keeping of other records that it deems appropriate.

Typically, the secretary and assistant secretaries are elected by the board of directors. Other members of the secretarial staff may be permanent employees of the corporation. One common avenue for a lawyer to become a corporate secretary is to handle corporate work for a company while serving as outside counsel.

Purchasing and Contract Administration Departments

It may seem a little odd to combine purchasing, which is the assembling of supplies, equipment, and services essential to the company's production, and contract administration, which is concerned with the sale of products. Yet in reality they are closely related, because both involve developing and monitoring of contracts.

One of the important roles that lawyers can and do play in the purchasing and sales areas relates to the "battle of the fine print," that is, the difficulties that all buyers and sellers have with the terms and conditions of purchase orders and the terms and conditions of sales. The working out of differences, and in many instances the development of basic agreements between purchasers and sellers, becomes a function in which legal training plays an important role.

Likewise, the development of an understanding by managers, buyers, and sales staff on the effects of "fine print" disputes cannot simply be left to those with legal training in purchasing and sales departments. To be effective on the job, you must understand the clauses in the company's contracts. Frequently, when contract terms are in dispute, it falls to the contract administration department to resolve the problem without litigation. More and more companies view adversarial dispute resolution as a failure of the highest order.

In the purchasing area, responsibility encompasses a variety of activities. Because the sums involved may run in the millions of dollars, a company seeks bids from suppliers based on the specifications of one or more departments within the company. Frequently it is necessary to survey a vendor's facilities and assess production capacity, quality control, and financial status to determine whether the vendor can meet the specifications.

When the supply contract has been completed, the purchasing area monitors conformance to delivery and cost schedules. If technical problems arise, the purchasing function serves as the coordinating unit between the vendor and the various company departments involved in the purchase.

Contract administration is closely allied to the sales and marketing functions. In some companies, the work is also split into commercial and government areas. The essential function, however, remains the same: monitoring the execution of the company's contracts for price, performance, and schedules.

Accomplishing this goal requires coordination with purchasing, production, quality assurance, and engineering functions. Records and reports may need to be prepared for customers, and contract modifications may have to be negotiated. This area of responsibility alone can be tremendously complex. Consider, for example, the complexities involved in the monitoring of a single contract for the development of an experimental aircraft for the U.S. Department of Defense.

In addition, this area may be responsible for the gathering of data for bid proposals and may analyze all major bids to determine why the company was not awarded the contract, as well as recommend procedures to be used in winning future contracts. Such data are extremely useful to the marketing department. Close coordination with the financial and credit areas is also essential.

▼▼▼▼▼

Gabe worked at a firm specializing in labor law after graduating from law school. One of his clients was a company with a large physical plant. When an opening in the legal department of the corporation came up, Gabe was the first choice for the job. He enjoyed the transition from law firm to in-house counsel. After working in the legal department on labor-relations and physical plant issues for a few years, Gabe decided to apply for the position of vice president of the physical plant when the current vice president took a job at another company. The position was a high-level management position overseeing the maintenance of the physical plant, acquisition of new facilities, and the procurement of all of the materials used by all of the departments to run the company and the plant facilities. The position reported directly to the president. Gabe was hired. The position gave Gabe a lot more responsibility and visibility within the company. Gabe's legal background helped him move into his current position and should be an asset as he continues to move up in the company.

Marketing Department

This area is the cornerstone upon which the company bases its whole existence. Without the sale of its products or services, the very reason for the existence of the company—earning a profit—disappears.

The marketing strategy used by a company varies widely, depending upon whether the customer is an individual, a corporation, or the government. Other significant factors in the marketing plan include the cost of the product or service, the transportation required to get the product to market, and the geographic appeal of the product. Nevertheless, all marketing involves several basic functions:

- ◆ Analyzing the market—Who are the customers for the company's products or services? Are there other consumers, not yet identified, for whom the company's products or services might be useful or desirable? What are the customer's specific needs and how do the company's products or services meet that need? Answers to these and related questions must be found.

◆ Choosing a marketing approach—Decide upon the best approach to both the present and the potential market. This process may involve studying competitors' strategies, keeping aware of new developments within one's own company that may be of interest to the customer, developing a media advertising program, and keeping in close contact with key personnel in the offices of potential customers.

◆ Staffing the marketing plan—Develop and monitor staff support for the strategy decided upon. This activity may involve employing an advertising agency and development of a field sales force and sales training programs.

Until very recently, only a handful of lawyers had chosen to work in the marketing area, possibly because of an oversimplified idea of the responsibilities involved. Now, however, many companies are eagerly seeking legally trained persons in an effort to avoid antitrust or regulatory compliance problems. One recent example may illustrate the reasons for this new attitude:

An advertising agency contracted with a federal government department to produce some films, a type of account they had not had before. Industry custom and union contracts dictated that those involved in the filming would be flown to the site in first class. The government contract, however, specified that first-class air travel was permitted only in highly exceptional circumstances. The conflict was not noted and upon the completion of the assignment, the advertising agency billed the government department in line with its customary commercial account practice. It took more than a year to get the matter straightened out. An account executive with legal training might well have been expected to be alert to such a potential conflict so that the problem could have been cleared up before it developed.

▼▼▼▼▼

Carrie had worked on several political campaigns before attending law school. She had worked with the public relations and marketing teams helping to create the candidate's image and presenting that image to the public. She stopped working on campaigns when she started law school. Carrie kept in contact with her political friends while she attended law school. During her second summer, Carrie took an internship at a large sports marketing firm. She thought it would be a fun way to spend the summer, and the firm was eager to have someone with Carrie's background and contacts. After the summer, the firm offered Carrie a job in its marketing department. Following law school, Carrie moved to the Midwest to work for the firm. After two years at the firm, Carrie was ready to move to the East Coast to take advantage of her political connections. She accepted a job in marketing at a securities firm. She was hired because of her high-end marketing experience and her political connections. After working for one year at the firm, Carrie was offered a position with a consulting firm. She took the consulting position so that she could have better control of her work schedule. She loves the flexibility of working as a consultant as a partner in the firm. Carrie has no regrets about never practicing law, but she believes her legal education has helped her in every position she has held.

Security Department

If the word *security* conjures up a picture of a lone guard at a plant gate, you are undoubtedly wondering why this category has been included here. Actually, the plant guard is only one type of visible evidence of the vast area of responsibility of the security department, which must develop and monitor a program that protects company property and equipment from theft.

Far less visible but certainly essential today is the protection of company documents and data, and in recent years this problem has become increasingly complex. Thus, current concerns include protection against computer data theft by unauthorized persons with sufficient technical knowledge to tie themselves into the company's network and the possibility of massive credit card counterfeiting. Prevention of industrial espionage has become a major area of corporate concern.

If the company is involved in the manufacture of products or the processing of material or data for the federal government, compliance with federal security regulations must also be planned and monitored. Consultation with government officials may be necessary to obtain interpretations of these rules, and requests for deviations may be necessary where undue hardship is involved.

In the long run, the effectiveness of security procedures is no better than their execution by the personnel working directly with sensitive areas. Thus, the company must produce manuals and conduct training sessions to inform personnel of their duties and responsibilities. Frequent rechecks are necessary to ensure that laxness in procedures does not occur due to a passage of time without an incident.

In a world of growing technological sophistication, security involves both physical safety and electronic considerations. Because of significant changes in investigative tools and new threats from security breaches, electronic surveillance has become big business. Security personnel must understand the technological elements, and they must be sensitive to privacy and other legal issues. Hence, legal training can be very useful.

A lawyer who is staff assistant to the head of the security department of a large insurance company, for instance, needs to know how to investigate security problems; how to detect crimes; how to deal with customers and employees suspected of irregularities without getting the company involved in false arrests or litigation; and how to assist police, the FBI, and district and U.S. attorneys in the handling of investigations and prosecutions. In this position he or she may have to know as much about criminal law and procedure as a good prosecutor does.

As business and industry grow ever more complex, so do their protection needs. Because many law students have law enforcement experience, they may have a decided advantage in the field of corporate security. Lawyers working in this area are sure to find new challenges to their skills and inventiveness.

▼▼▼▼▼

Dan joined the FBI right out of law school. After traveling around the United States from assignment to assignment, he decided that he wanted to have a more stable home life. With his law degree and his FBI training, Dan was very employable as the head of security for a major corporation. Following the tragedies on September 11, 2001, all major corporations reevaluated their internal and external security programs. Dan decided to leave the FBI to work for a major corporation as the vice president of corporate security. Although the position requires Dan to travel to all of the corporate locations, he works out of the headquarters office and doesn't have to travel as much as he did as an FBI field agent. Dan's law degree helped at the FBI, and it will help him as a corporate vice president when he balances the company's need for security with the individual employee's rights of privacy.

Information Technology Department

The computer revolution has given rise to an entire new field of work in business and industry: information technology (IT), sometimes referred to as knowledge management (KM). At one time IT was just someone who came around and fixed your computer when it wouldn't boot up. Today, however, IT professionals are involved in every facet of virtually every organization. They order and install the most appropriate hardware and software for the company's needs. They deal with ongoing problems like obsolescence, compatibility, and viruses. They may manage the company's Web site and other online resources. They are frequently responsible for training system users and troubleshooting problems. They frequently face copyright and trademark questions involving electronic publications. They may even be involved in the highest levels of the company in strategic planning.

Although most lawyers are not themselves IT professionals, a surprising number possess skills in both law and information technology. Some of these lawyers may choose to work on the technology side of a company rather than on the legal side. In view of the level of technological sophistication of most law students compared with that of law graduates of only a few years ago, this is not a surprising development.

▼▼▼▼▼

While Janice was in law school, she worked as a computer-assisted legal research company representative and assisted in the school's computer lab. She was interested in intellectual property law and thought she would work for an intellectual property firm when she graduated. After passing the bar, Janice did not get a job with one of the very few firms she applied to. Janice realized that she was too selective in her search, but she did not want to take a job in an area where she would not enjoy the subject matter of the law. Janice had stayed in touch with the director of information technology at her law school and accepted an hourly, consulting position when one of the undergraduate student workers graduated and left the position. Two years later, Janice is the associate director of information technology and a full-time employee of the university. Janice has not totally given up the idea of practicing intellectual property law, but she is enjoying herself working on campus and getting paid to work with computers.

Intellectual Property Department

Copyright, trademark, trade secrets, patents, and other aspects of intellectual property (IP) law are not new areas of practice. Companies are recognizing, however, that protection of their IP rights can be critical to the future of their business. In some fields, inventions have transformed (and in some cases are still transforming) consumer products. These include pharmaceuticals, health care, communications, and, of course, technology companies. There was a time when the IP section was a backwater in the corporate legal department, but increasingly IP operates as a separate department. It may be a stretch to call IP work nonlegal, but the work involves much more than just filing and defending patents, copyrights, and trademarks.

▼▼▼▼▼

Lauren worked for a large law firm in the intellectual property department. She handled title searches for television and movie scripts, trademark and trade name searches, and worked with her entertainment and nonentertainment company clients to protect their intellectual property in the United States and abroad. She spent a great deal of time preparing cease-and-desist letters for her clients in their efforts to police their marks on the Internet. Although Lauren loved the work, she hated the hours. As an associate in the firm, she was required to bill more than two thousand hours a year. One of her nonentertainment clients, a toy manufacturer, was having a difficult time keeping up with policing its marks. The general counsel asked Lauren whether she would like to move to a smaller town, work more reasonable hours, and get paid about half of what she was making at the firm. Lauren decided that an in-house position working forty to fifty hours a week would be a great way to practice the type of law she loved at a company with stock options and growth potential. Lauren took the job and loves it. She does both legal and nonlegal work. She enjoys her management position, and she chooses when to handle a legal problem or when to hire outside counsel. All of the litigation is farmed out to law firms. Lauren would not go back to the firm for any amount of money. She is happy with her income and her lifestyle.

Securities Companies and Banks

Positions in the financial area are not confined solely to industry. Opportunities can be found in the nation's banks, financial institutions, investment houses, and brokerage firms. It is becoming common for a bank's trust officers to have legal training. As a consequence of the complex legal requirements for trust administration, a lawyer is ideally suited for the position.

Other positions where legal training is helpful include commercial loan officers, mortgage officers, loan counselors, and foreign-exchange traders. Although these positions have not traditionally required any formal legal training, as the banking industry consolidates, new jobs may begin to go to the individuals with a legal background and a desire to work in a bank. During the 1980s, when mergers and acquisitions work was at its peak, many investment banks contracted directly with large law firms to hire legal talent. Although the mergers and acquisitions frenzy subsided in the early 1990s, the acceptance of lawyers in banking circles has remained.

Banks, insurance companies, brokerage firms, and investment houses often employ the services of financial analysts. These individuals interpret data concerning investments, price, yield, stability, and future trends, drawing information from daily stock and bond reports, financial periodicals, securities manuals, and personal interviews. They summarize data setting forth current and long-term trends in investment risks and measurable economic influences pertinent to the status of investments. In some instances, they may transmit buy-and-sell orders to brokers based on their analysis. Legal training can be an asset, but the job also requires a background in economics.

Account representatives who sell financial products to the public also benefit from legal training. Understanding and explaining investment instruments to clients requires financial and legal training, combined with excellent communication skills. With a legal background, a successful and aggressive account representative may move rapidly up the corporate ladder.

▼▼▼▼▼

Adam decided to go to law school to give himself options. He was a licensed Series 7 broker before law school and continued to work during law school. Adam went to school part time so that he could afford it. Although he didn't have any specific plans to practice law when he began law school, he found that he enjoyed the intellectual challenge of school. Nevertheless, he didn't want to do what the lawyers in the case studies were doing. Law school convinced Adam to stick with the securities business. Following law school, Adam decided to use his degree to lower his daily stress level by taking a job as a compliance officer for his brokerage firm. Adam enjoys the regular hours and steady pay, along with the reduced stress. He couldn't have made the transition without a law degree.

Compliance officers serve as in-house co⟨
and brokerage firms. They review public offeri
supervise the preparation of periodic reports ⟨
the National Association of Securities Dealers
Stock Exchange. They also monitor the capital ⟨
compliance with the exchange minimums.

▼▼▼▼▼

Doug worked as a floor trader before law school. He left his
position to lower the stress level in his life. After law school, he
worked for a law firm in their securities department. For Doug,
the law firm work was too tame. Doug craved the excitement of
the stock market but he did not want the stress of a floor trader.
Doug decided to join a securities firm as a stockbroker. For him, it
was a good compromise between the law firm and floor trading.
He had the hours and excitement of trading, but not the minute-
by-minute pressure. Law school and Doug's law firm contacts
helped him build a great book of business in a very short amount
of time.

Insurance Companies

Insurance companies employ individuals with legal training in all
aspects of the industry. Salespersons, adjusters, administrators,
lobbyists, and lawyers work in every important area within the
industry.

One major difference between in-house corporate insurance
work and working for an insurance company as outside counsel is
that, as in-house counsel, you have only one client—the corporation—and the department is viewed as a cost center. Although
some insurance company positions are similar, the sales positions
and account executive positions are considered revenue centers
where pay may be based on performance.

Many insurance companies use a special entry-level position
to thoroughly acquaint new additions to their staff with the special
problems, procedures, and policies peculiar to the insurance
industry, and to the specific company. This position is commonly
known as claims adjustor.

A claims adjustor investigates claims for loss and damage filed conjunction with a specific insurance policy and tries to negotiate an out-of-court settlement. He or she examines the claim form and other records to determine insurance coverage, interviews or corresponds with the claimant and witnesses, consults police and hospital records, and inspects property damage to determine the extent of the company's liability, varying the method of investigation according to the type of insurance.

The adjuster prepares a report of the findings and seeks to negotiate a settlement with the claimant. When a settlement cannot be negotiated, the claims adjustor makes a recommendation for litigation to the legal department. Although he or she is not directly involved in the litigation, the claims adjustor may attend the litigation hearing.

The claims adjustor generally does not settle life or accident-and-sickness claims. The individual's title may be designated, however, according to the type of claim with which he or she deals, such as casualty insurance, fidelity and surety bonds, fire insurance, or marine insurance.

These positions give day-to-day experience with the practical implementation of the company's insurance programs, and they provide a unique opportunity to observe firsthand the various opportunities for advancement to positions peculiar to industry operations.

One such position is that of underwriter. The duties of an underwriter include reviewing insurance applications to evaluate the degree of risk involved and accepting those that follow the company's underwriting policies. The underwriter reviews company records to determine the amount of insurance in force on a single risk or a group of closely related risks and evaluates the possibility of losses due to catastrophe or excessive insurance. Risks that are too high are declined, or reinsurance may be authorized. If the risk is substantial, the underwriter may limit the company's obligation by decreasing the value of the policy, specifying applicable endorsements, or applying a rating to ensure safe and profitable distribution or risks. Underwriters will usually work in a single area such as accident and sickness, automobile, bond, fire, liability, life, marine, property, or special risks.

Individuals with legal training are also found frequently in the local and district offices of insurance companies. Often they will start in sales to become familiar with the potential insurance needs of the clients. Legal training may prove helpful for explaining most effectively how the recommended coverage will specifically answer the client's needs. Law school-educated people are also used in selecting and writing endorsements and riders, reviewing policies to be sure that the correct coverage is included, and, perhaps even more importantly, participating in the handling of insurance claims.

▼▼▼▼▼

Ed was an insurance salesman before he decided to go to law school. To pay the bills, he continued to sell insurance while he was in law school. While he enjoyed the law school experience, he decided that he did not want to practice law when he graduated. During his third year of law school, Ed decided that he would continue selling insurance for his old company. He used his law school alumni directory to expand his list of contacts and enjoys working his own hours. In retrospect, Ed is not sure whether he would attend law school knowing what he now knows. In any event, the contacts have been wonderful for his insurance business.

Health Care and Pharmaceutical Companies

Concern with rising health care costs has brought a new dimension to the administrative functions of health care institutions. Cost containment is a complicated matter that combines many legal and administrative problems. (See the discussion of in-house health care management above.)

Managed health care, pharmaceutical manufacturing, medical research, nursing, and hospice care are multibillion-dollar industries. These fields are in constant contact with the legal system. Yet, as lawyers, we often don't think of this vast infrastructure; we see only the cases generated by health care litigation. We should recognize,

▼▼▼▼▼

Hillary Clinton, a lawyer, took it upon herself to reform health care delivery during the 1990s while she served as first lady. As a senator from New York, she has continued her crusade for afford-able health care. With the rapid changes in the delivery of health care through health maintenance organizations, new challenges in health care management require administrators who under-stand the management and legal issues that must be addressed to compete in a new environment.

however, that these industries represent a huge source of jobs, par-ticularly for individuals with prelegal experiences in these fields.

Labor costs, materials costs, liability costs, and administra-tive costs must be controlled and well managed if affordable health care is to be delivered. Government cuts in research grants must be replaced with private funds. Cuts in insurance coverage for par-ticular treatments and cuts in Medicare and other social programs must be considered in the management of a health care institution to ensure its survival in the future.

All major health care facilities employ professional fundrais-ers to solicit funds for the institution. Planned gifts are an increas-ing source of revenue for research and health care organizations. (See the fundraising discussion in Chapter 9.)

Although many doctors and scientists write their own research grant proposals, some institutions employ a grant writer or hire a freelance grant writer to assist in the process.

Pharmaceutical companies employ people with legal training in positions ranging from sales, to contract administration, to patent registration, to regulatory compliance, and to general admin-istration. Some positions require the services of practicing lawyers, either as in-house or outside counsel. Others do not involve the practice of law; they merely draw upon the knowledge acquired during your apprenticeship into the profession.

Despite the many changes and controversies involving health care in recent years, the health care industry has remained strong.

It constitutes one of the largest industries in the United States and is a significant growth area in the national economy. It should come as no surprise that many health care professionals pursue a legal education just to be able to cope with the legal issues that confront their organizations.

Real Estate Sales and Development Companies

Real estate sales and development constitute one of the two largest groups of employers of lawyers. (Investment banking and securities sales is the other major group that hires lawyers who have left the practice or who have never practiced law.) Real estate sales and development offers entrepreneurial as well as corporate opportunities.

As a real estate sales agent, your legal background allows you to simplify the forms, or at least the explanation of the forms, for your clients. In addition, you can use your creativity to draft sales contracts that meet the needs of both parties, including financial terms that allow the parties to complete the transaction. From a successful sales career, you may move up into management where your experience and education are beneficial. Interestingly, a fair number of law graduates with real estate experience return to the field after graduation, using their legal knowledge and skill to leverage their work with more sophisticated transactions.

As a developer, your education can assist you in zoning-regulation compliance or in meeting the regulatory requirements necessary for a variance. Your ability to negotiate favorable construction contracts from the various subcontractors on a major project may save your company money and help keep projects on schedule. Understanding local government, and how to move your projects through the regulatory agencies necessary for approval in a timely manner, can save a significant amount of money in lost time and opportunities. Many major development companies are owned by lawyers or employ individuals with legal training to assist in the daily work of the company. Your education should open doors if you are interested in a career in real estate sales or development. In many states, residential real estate closings are handled by, or supplemented by, title insurance companies. Many such companies are owned and staffed by lawyers.

▼▼▼▼▼

Wendy managed her parents' apartments while she was in law school. She didn't like attending to plumbing emergencies at 3 A.M., but she did enjoy the administrative work. Working in a law firm never appealed to her, so she decided to pursue her property management career. After she graduated and passed the bar, she looked for jobs with the major property managers in town. Although the company thought she was overqualified for the job, they decided to take a chance on her because she had property management experience. Wendy moved up in the company and now works in the property development and acquisitions department. Her law degree has been very helpful so far.

High-Tech Companies

High-tech companies continue to evolve as Internet commerce and digital media develop. Although the dot-com bubble of the 1990s has burst, companies that are able to develop or take advantage of ever-emerging advances in technology continue to prosper. New companies are being created to take advantage of these expanding opportunities. Companies involved in high technology are similar to engineering companies with regard to their needs for lawyers and individuals with legal training (see the "Engineering Firms" section in Chapter 10).

In addition to the need for government contract administrators and general administrators, high-tech firms need in-house advice on patent protection for their inventions and product improvements. Patent practice is a highly specialized area of the law, though someone with a high-tech background could move into a quasi-legal position that would include patent review and legal contract administration if outside counsel were employed for formal patent prosecutions. A technical or scientific background is essential for a position in this area. In addition to the need for people with a background in technology, lawyers with trademark and copyright experience are needed to protect the intellectual property of the company.

Security is a major concern for high-tech companies. Companies must guard against industrial espionage by competitors and foreign countries. Elaborate security measures are required for certain types of governmental work. Security experts are in demand in the high-tech field. (See the discussion above on corporate security for more information in this area.)

A high-tech company that is considering a public stock offering could benefit from corporate officers with SEC experience. Understanding the procedures and paperwork involved with a public stock offering can save the company some attorney's fees if the work is handled in-house. A background in debt and equity financing can be invaluable for any startup company.

▼▼▼▼▼

Andrea graduated from law school with an idea for starting an Internet business. She formed a partnership with a friend, and the two of them started construction of their Web site. Andrea filed the company's articles of incorporation and started to raise money, while her friend continued to design the Web site. Andrea sold the idea to a venture capital fund that invested a significant amount of money in the company. The venture capital fund replaced Andrea and her friend as corporate officers when the Web site started to have functional design problems. Andrea and her friend left their company with worthless stock, a nice savings-account balance, and great experience. After her initial failure, Andrea found another startup Internet company that needed her legal and management skills. Andrea took an equity position in the company in lieu of salary for the first six months of operations. The company seems to be viable, and Andrea is hoping it will succeed.

During the 1990s, the dot-com revolution produced a wave of new Internet service companies. Although many of the early entrants in this new economy experienced financial difficulties, and many of them failed, this is not unusual for any new industry. Internet companies continue to grow as a segment of the larger economy. Lawyers are often involved with these startups, not just as counsel, but as entrepreneurs; not just for legal advice, but for other services as well.

High-tech companies continue to hire lawyers for in-house legal positions and for business affairs positions. They function much like media companies. High technology will continue to provide employment opportunities for lawyers who want to practice law, and for those who don't.

Energy Companies

Natural resources and energy are depletable resources. Many energy resources such as oil, gas, and coal have finite reserves. Others, like nuclear energy, foster enormous controversy. Some energy sources, such as solar power, have not been developed to the point where they are available to consumers. Whatever your personal feelings are about energy resources, you have to admit that energy issues will remain critical for the foreseeable future.

Lawyers have always been involved in the energy business, from securing the rights to oil, gas, and minerals to developing the legal framework for exploiting these resources and delivering them to consumers. In today's global economy, these activities become more complex and protracted. Legal problems permeate the energy industry, so it follows that legal training will always prove to be an asset for those who pursue careers in this field.

Government Service

8

Government agencies hire hundreds of lawyers for both legal and nonlegal positions every time a presidential administration changes. Although the numbers are reduced as the governmental entity becomes more local, states, counties, and cities go through the same hiring process with each governmental administration change.

The largest number of federal jobs is in Washington, D.C., although there are federal jobs in all fifty states, including the territories. State and local jobs exist in almost every city and town with a concentration of positions located in the state capitol and the county seats.

Executive Branch

Many United States presidents have been lawyers. Because of this background, presidents have hired many lawyers who leave practice or business to serve in the executive branch of the government. Many cabinet and subcabinet posts are filled by lawyers because of the training and connections established in school and after graduation. The president relies on advisors—both lawyers and nonlawyers—to run various segments of the government and to keep him or her apprised of the activities of their departments.

These positions are generally filled by political appointees. Typically, the president fills the positions with people who have been loyal to the candidate and the party during the campaign. Although ability and credentials are important to the positions, political connections are critical for the top jobs. Lower-level jobs are filled by those with the greatest ability.

▼▼▼▼▼

Janice was active in the Republican Party while attending college and law school. During law school, she received a scholarship that introduced her to prominent members of the Republican Party. She was invited to attend the local fundraisers and meet the most prominent party patrons. Following graduation from law school, she returned to her home state to work for a startup dot-com company. She started in the general counsel's office handling name clearances for Internet Web sites, trademark filings, and whatever else she was assigned. She worked there for a couple of years until she was approached by another Internet start-up company to serve as general counsel. She took the job and left her successful company for the opportunity to participate in a startup venture. The company developed an interesting niche market but failed to generate enough income to keep the company viable. The owners found a buyer, and Janice negotiated the buyout of the company and the phasing out of her job. After one successful Internet adventure and one unsuccessful Internet experience, Janice contacted her old friends in the Republican Party, who were gearing up for a presidential campaign. She was hired as a paid campaign worker and worked to get her candidate elected. Following the campaign, she received an appointment to work in the Department of Energy. She has worked there ever since her candidate was elected six years ago. When her employment ends, she plans to find a job with one of the many companies that she has dealt with during the course of her tenure at the Department of Energy.

The executive branch has agencies to direct every facet of government that is the constitutional responsibility of the president. Individuals with legal training are employed at all levels of the agencies, as lawyers as well as as administrators or bureaucrats. Contact your local representative or senator for job availability information.

State executive branch jobs are filled in the same manner as federal jobs. Political patronage is more important at the local government level than at the federal level. Consult your local politicians for job availability information.

Law Enforcement Agencies

The Federal Bureau of Investigation, the Central Intelligence Agency, the National Security Agency, the Bureau of Alcohol, Tobacco and Firearms, the Department of the Treasury (which includes the United States Customs Service), federal and state marshals, and state and local police departments all recruit people with legal training to serve in individual law enforcement organizations. A law degree should accelerate your promotions through the ranks as long as you possess the other skills necessary to perform and advance. In fact, FBI agents are drawn almost exclusively from the ranks of lawyers and CPAs. (For example, Elliott Ness, the leader of the "Untouchables" who brought down gangster Al Capone for tax evasion, was a lawyer.)

Diplomatic Agencies

Travel to exotic lands has always been the appeal for those who dream of a career in the foreign diplomatic corps. Some posts are more desirable than others, though all diplomats have the opportunity to travel and possibly to influence world politics. Outside of an assignment to the United Nations in New York, the majority of the positions are in the capital cities and major tourist destinations in foreign countries around the world. The foreign diplomatic corps offers an excellent opportunity to see the world.

At the highest levels, Foreign Service representatives are political appointees. The ambassadors and chargés d'affaires are appointed by the president; the remaining posts in the foreign services are generally filled by career diplomats. Legal training is an asset that can enhance your chances of becoming a member of the foreign diplomatic corps. Fluency in at least one foreign language is generally required for a foreign post. Competition for positions in the diplomatic corps is very high.

Intelligence Agencies

The Central Intelligence Agency and other intelligence agencies operate to gather political, economic, military, and other intelligence. Although we sometimes think of intelligence work as spying and covert espionage, in truth much of the work is meticulous research, analysis, and interpretation. The events of September 11, 2001, illustrate the critical need for good intelligence. As with law enforcement, legal training may prove to be an excellent background for this kind of work.

Regulatory Agencies

There is a governmental agency to regulate just about every aspect of our lives. If the agency does not exist on the federal level, state or local government has probably formed an agency to regulate the activity.

Regulatory agencies can develop, draft, and implement their own regulations when authorized by law. Because of the nature of the agencies, individuals with legal training are naturals to perform in the quasi-legal regulatory positions.

Regulatory boards are appointed by the chief executive. Except for the political appointees, the board members hire their staffs. Legislative drafters, legislative analysts, regulatory compliance officers, and general administrators are required to conduct the agencies' business.

Although some of these positions have been filled by individuals with legal training in the past, there is no reason why more of these positions should not be filled by lawyers. Significantly, many lawyers who begin their government careers in strictly legal jobs find that as they move up the administrative ladder, they do less and less legal work, until at the highest levels their work is almost exclusively nonlegal.

Judicial Branch

Practicing lawyers with political connections may be appointed to a judgeship by the executive in office. Besides the judicial positions, judges hire clerks to perform their research. They also hire court administrators and other court personnel. These lower-level positions are generally not filled by people with legal training, but there is no reason why a particular position could not be filled by a lawyer.

Court clerks are often lawyers who prefer administrative duties rather than the practice of law. Career clerks run a judge's courtroom and supervise the workflow to keep the court efficient. These positions offer the clerk regular hours while keeping the clerk involved with the administration of justice. See *The Legal Career Guide: From Law Student to Lawyer,* by Gary A. Munneke (ABA, 2002).

Legislative Branch

No discussion of nonlegal careers in government would be complete without mentioning the legislative branch. Congress, state legislatures, city and county governments, local boards, and other quasi-legislative bodies benefit from the participation of lawyers. Legal skills are useful in persuading others to follow particular courses of action. Legal analysis and drafting abilities help to assure that legislation accomplishes the intent of the legislative body and not fail because of constitutional infirmity. Lawyer participation in the legislative branch goes far beyond elected officials to include the countless staffers who work behind the scenes.

The contacts made during law school and practice can serve as an excellent source for campaign staff and patrons. Successful classmates can provide donations and introductions to their clients who would like to support a candidate who is accessible and recommended by a trusted counselor. The alumni directory is a logical starting point for any political campaign organizing. Legal training is an asset for a member of a legislative body.

The Military

All of the military services recruit law students to enter their individual branches as lawyers. Although these positions are legal positions, it is possible to use the commission to move up through the ranks and out of the legal services division or Judge Advocate General (JAG) Corps.

When you enter the military as a lawyer, you do so as an officer. As with any other job, an advanced degree can help you as you move out of the legal department and into the upper ranks of management. Consult your local branch military recruiter for a personal discussion on the opportunities available to someone with your particular background. In addition, some legally trained individuals may move through the ranks completely outside the JAG Corps.

▼▼▼▼▼

Shannon joined the JAG Corps immediately following law school. She was sent to basic training and JAG school to learn about life in the military and military law. After completion of JAG school, she was sent to a military base to prosecute soldiers who violated military laws. She was able to get in the courtroom in months, rather than years, as it would have taken had she been on a traditional law-firm path. During the Gulf War, she was selected to serve as a mayor of a city; JAG officers become the government in cities seized in war. Since her Gulf War experience, she has moved up in rank and assumed more administrative duties at each new base assignment. Shannon is happy with her job and comfortable as a military officer. The only part she still doesn't like is marching with her rifle!

Public and Community Service

9

A number of possibilities exist in associations and related organizations for legally trained individuals. Most associations are nonprofit organizations and need legal expertise to maintain their status and comply with annual filing requirements. These groups often consider a legal background helpful, if not necessary, to their work. As the role of private associations and institutions evolves over the years, employees with legal backgrounds become assets in guiding the various operations. Although other qualifications are necessary for the positions, legal training enhances a candidate's appeal and can make a significant difference in performance. Once a lawyer is hired for a particular position, many organizations seek other lawyers, sometimes to the exclusion of nonlawyers who held the position previously. For a comprehensive guide to associations and institutions, see Gale Research Company's *Encyclopedia of Associations.*

Professional Associations

Professional associations, including bar associations, other professional and occupation-related societies, trade associations, sports associations, and hobby associations, are organizations that provide benefits to members, whether the members are individuals, organizations, or both. Most of these organization have tax-exempt status.

The term *association* is widely used, though many organizations identify themselves as leagues, societies, fraternities, alliances, or institutes. All are essentially the same type of organization. They are formed to advance the interests of their members.

An association's staff serves essentially as a secretariat for the organization and can vary in number from one person to hundreds. Staff size determines the nature of the particular opportunity, be it the Jack-of-all-trades of the one-person staff or the specialized role required on a large staff. Someone who is able to work with the board of directors, association employees, and volunteers is invaluable to an association.

The services provided to members include administrative management of the organization and dissemination of information relating to the special interests of the group. Services may also include fundraising, legislative review, lobbying, meeting planning, contract negotiation, developing educational seminars, and membership promotion.

Organizational structures vary widely depending on the size of the association and the nature of its activities. The work holds particular appeal for lawyers because their legal skills are often directly applicable, and the individual interests and hobbies of the lawyers may be represented by the organizations.

PACs, Lobbying, and Campaigns

A political action committee (PAC) is a tax-exempt nonprofit national organization formed to fund the campaigns of candidates who have viewpoints similar to the PAC's constituency. PACs are generally established to address a single issue important to the constituency. Although many are focused on individual rights issues, some have adopted platforms that correspond to one of the political parties' political agendas. Because the main function of PACs is to influence candidates by funding campaigns in circumvention of the campaign fundraising laws, they can exert a great deal of influence with their dollars. They must engage in active fundraising, campaigning, and lobbying to fulfill their purposes.

Lobbying organizations differ from PACs in that they are generally tied to specific businesses, industries, or labor organizations rather than individual issues or political platforms. Lobbying organizations contribute to candidates who support the organizations' positions regardless of the candidate's political party affiliation. They tend to focus less on individual rights issues and more on business legislation that affects their industry.

Campaigns are organized to promote an individual candidate by raising funds, coordinating favorable publicity, and soliciting votes. Successful campaigns continue after the candidate has been elected. The campaign committee continues to work to keep the elected official in the public eye, raise funds for the next campaign, and assist the elected official's staff in providing services to the constituency.

PACs, lobbying organizations, and campaigns all hire legally trained people to serve as legal counsel and in nonlegal positions. The larger organizations can afford to hire professional staff, but they all rely on volunteer staffing.

Perhaps the best way to develop the skills (and credentials) necessary to obtain paid positions in political campaigns is to spend time in the trenches as a volunteer. Most small organizations rely solely on volunteer staff. Because each organization must comply with national and local campaign laws, legal expertise is required. In addition, each group is organized as a nonprofit organization and must comply with the laws that pertain to the establishment and maintenance of nonprofits.

Professional fundraisers are employed to solicit income for the groups. Lobbyists are hired by PACs and lobbying organizations, though campaigns are generally staffed by people seeking positions with the candidate once he or she is elected. Legal training is helpful in performing effectively in all of these positions.

National and International Service Organizations

There are thousands of national service organizations representing many charitable and environmental causes. They include the American Cancer Society, the Optimists Club, the Kiwanis Club, the United Way, the League of Women Voters, the Boy Scouts of America, the Girl Scouts of America, the American Association of Retired Persons, the Sierra Club, and Habitat for Humanity, to name just a few. All are organized as tax-exempt nonprofit corporations.

International service organizations include groups such as Rotary International, the Red Cross, the Organization of American States, Amnesty International, Greenpeace, and the United Nations (UN), including the specialized agencies of the UN such as the International Monetary Fund (IMF), the United Nations Educational, Scientific and Cultural Organization (UNESCO), and the World Health Organization (WHO).

The constituency for these organizations is made up of local clubs or groups, which are primarily involved in service activities within their community. The central office coordinates individual groups and provides them with educational, promotional, fundraising, and other support activities and performs the general administrative functions necessary to the health and well-being of any organization.

It is difficult to list the administrative and employment needs of the various national and international service organizations. Because of the broad scope of the international organizations, they may have complex logistical management issues. The basic need for specific job functions, however, remains the same, even though the nature of the service activities varies widely.

Although legal training is helpful in all levels of management, it is not usually a prerequisite for the job. Management experience is generally the most important skill in coordinating the various facets of these organizations. Legal training can be helpful when dealing with multistate or multinational organizations. Most large organizations have in-house counsel to advise on regulatory compliance, though a legally trained manager should be able to understand the various requirements and assist counsel in avoiding unnecessary business complications.

Unions

Unions represent workers in almost every type of nonmanagerial activity in business, industry, and government. Although all unions use lawyers on a regular basis, many are finding that individuals with legal training bring an important background to administrative positions. Moving up through the ranks is no longer a prerequisite for consideration for union posts, though active union membership before, during, or after law school may open doors for lawyers in this area.

Representing members in arbitrations is generally done by union representatives. A lawyer with a background in labor law and alternative dispute resolution could be an asset to the union as a grievance arbitrator.

Contract negotiation has traditionally been a function of union leadership. Tradition and industry standards have been the basis for new contracts. With geographical shifts in the work force, rising health-care costs, and advancing technology, reliance on past practices will not keep a union strong. Someone with legal training who is familiar with union traditions and industry standards may be an asset to the membership in negotiating a contract that preserves jobs for the membership, continues important benefits, and allows the company to make a profit in light of the demands of the marketplace.

One of the newer membership benefits being offered by unions is a group legal-service plan. In addition to the legal staff required to provide those services, there is a need for people to administer them. Someone with legal training is an obvious asset in the legal administrator's position.

▼▼▼▼▼

Grace worked at a labor law firm following graduation from law school. She enjoyed the issues, but she did not like the business side of practicing law. She wanted to avoid having to keep her hours and bill clients while she still worked with people to ensure that their workplaces were safe and that their rights were not violated. She had worked closely with several of the local unions on cases and knew most of the in-house lawyers. When one of her clients decided to expand the in-house legal department, Grace was asked to apply. She took the opportunity to move out of her law firm and into the union. The pay is slightly lower, but the hours were more reasonable and she no longer has to submit time sheets and bill clients. As an in-house lawyer, she participates in the grievance hearings and counsels union members. When the contract expires with management, she will participate in those negotiations as well.

Foundations and Charitable Organizations

Foundations and charitable organizations are established as a result of grants or endowments for a philanthropic purpose. They are often created by wealthy individuals for specific charitable, educational, informational, or research purposes. After they are established, they must manage the existing endowment and raise funds for future growth. These organizations need administrators, directors, and fundraisers.

Fundraising is becoming essential to private organizations as federal and state funding becomes more scarce. Many fundraising positions have been traditionally filled by professionals with financial and sales backgrounds, but lawyers and individuals with legal training are beginning to enter the profession. Legal training is necessary when counseling potential donors on the benefits of planned gifts, including charitable remainder trusts, unitrusts, pooled income funds, charitable gift annuities, and bequests.

Tax and estate planning knowledge are required to adequately advise both the institution and the donor. Many people consider fundraising a rewarding career because satisfaction comes from all facets of the gift. First, the gift helps the organization continue by providing it with the funds necessary to operate. Second, the donor's wishes to make a significant contribution to the organization are realized through the fundraiser's creative efforts. Fundraising is an important job that enables professionals to make meaningful contributions to an organization. Opportunities exist for individuals with the requisite expertise who are committed to a particular cause.

The complexity of administration offers unique possibilities for lawyers. Regulatory compliance to maintain tax-exempt status is a major concern of foundation and charitable organization administrators. In addition, a substantial portion of their work involves screening applications for grants and verifying the credentials of the grant seekers. Once a grant is given, some organizations continue to monitor the grantee to verify that the purposes of the grant are being fulfilled.

Foundations and charitable organizations employ professional fundraisers to solicit money actively for operating expenses and to increase the endowment for grants. Many professional fundraiser positions are being filled by lawyers who wish to use their training for the benefit of philanthropic causes.

Fundraising professionals must understand the various planned gift instruments, and the tax consequences of the gift to the donor, in order to advise potential donors. Many lawyers employed by associations and institutions view their work as both personally rewarding and as an important contribution to society as well. They play a vital role in helping service and charitable organizations advance their causes, and they are often instrumental in decisions about how the charity will distribute its largesse in the community.

Development and planned giving professionals are often lawyers or CPAs. Because the structuring of a planned gift oftentimes involves estate planning or the establishment of a trust or estate planning, legal training is an asset. Pledges and structured gifts involve contracts and tax planning. Although most organizations encourage their major donors to consult independent counsel, development professionals must be able to explain the transaction to potential donors and negotiate deal points with donors' lawyers.

▼▼▼▼▼

Ted was comfortable and fairly happy with his personal injury law practice. When his daughter was diagnosed with cancer, he became obsessed with cancer research and the quality of medical care his daughter received. After a year of chemotherapy, his daughter had a bone marrow transplant. Ted spent the nights with his daughter and worked during the day. His wife stayed with their daughter during the day. After their daughter was released from the hospital, Ted approached the hospital administration to find out about fundraising opportunities. He studied the various gift opportunities and researched the tax ramifications of planned gifts. Ted volunteered for several months, helping the fundraising staff identify prospects and ask for gifts. Ted found the work so rewarding that he decided to quit his law practice and become a full-time fundraiser. The hospital was preparing for a capital campaign and decided that Ted would be a good addition to the fundraising team. Ted never expected to change careers, but the opportunity presented itself and he took it. He did not realize how fulfilling a job could be until he changed jobs and started working for a cause that was dear to his heart.

▼▼▼▼▼

Alicia graduated from law school and took a job in the development office at her alma mater. She began in the major gifts group because of her legal background. In law school, Alicia took all of the tax and estate planning courses the school offered. She was hired to help with major gifts, and to help structure planned gifts. Although she always advises the donor to consult an independent lawyer and tax accountant concerning the gift, she prepares the transfer documents for the donor on behalf of the school. Alicia enjoys working with donors to help them make the most significant gifts they can afford and structuring them so donors receives the maximum benefit. Assisting the donors is rewarding work, and Alicia particularly enjoys helping her alma mater secure its future.

Professional Services

10

The concept of all professional services is that licensed professionals deliver specific services to individuals and organizations. Professional service firms are often smaller than industrial organizations that produce and market products, and typically a professional services firm will have a limited scope. For example, a law office will provide only legal services, whereas an engineering office will provide only engineering services.

Some professional service firms have experimented with multidisciplinary service offices, but they represent the exception, not the rule. A transition from a law practice to a professional service firm may be a logical step for lawyers looking to use their undergraduate training with their legal training in a corporate setting. It offers them the opportunity to combine their avocation with their vocation at the highest levels of professional service.

Accounting Firms

Once almost exclusively hiring accounting and business school graduates, accounting firms are increasingly finding that individuals with this specialized background who also have legal training expand the depth and quality of their services. Some of the biggest firms have added law-office management and other consulting departments.

Accounting and management procedures apply equally to law offices and to business organizations, though there are some substantial differences. The management of those differences can be of utmost importance to the individual law office in need of specialized consulting services.

In addition to the auditing work that these organizations routinely perform, they do a great deal of tax planning work, which has attracted a substantial number of lawyers to the field because of the legal issues involved. Most of these firms insist upon an accounting degree or a CPA certificate for employment. The structure of accounting firms is similar to that of a law firm, so there is the potential for partnership. Partnership is generally only granted to those with a CPA certificate, unless the accounting firm is structured as a multidisciplinary partnership (see the discussion of multiprofessional services in "Personal Financial Services" section on page 120).

When applying to these firms, it is important to make clear that you are applying for a nonlegal accounting position rather than a legal position. In seeking a nonlegal position, the firm will want to verify that you are truly interested in accounting and that they will not find themselves with a frustrated would-be lawyer on their hands. (For more information on internal departmental duties, see the "Tax Department" section in Chapter 7.)

A word about Enron: The 2001 collapse of the Enron Corporation raised substantial questions about the nature of accounting firms' work. If the same firm provides business consulting services, staffs a company's financial department, and audits a company's books, the Enron debacle suggests that accounting firms face serious conflict of interest issues. Notwithstanding these problems, however, look for the role of accounting firms in business advising to grow, and expect the number of lawyers who work for accounting firms to increase.

▼▼▼▼▼

Jerome was a tax partner in a major law firm in a midwestern city. After turning away countless calls from headhunters over the years, he was eventually intrigued by one call about a position with one of the leading accounting firms. When he interviewed with the firm, he learned that he would make more money and spend less time in the office than he did as a private practitioner. The CPA firm appeared to have resources his law firm could only dream about. It turned out to be an offer he could not refuse, and after twenty-seven years as a practicing lawyer, Jerome accepted the job with the accounting firm.

Health Care Organizations

Health care organizations like clinics and hospitals have traditionally been run by doctors and professional health care administrators. An understanding of medicine and medical procedure is essential to an understanding of the needs of the doctors, nurses, and patients who are treated at the facility. In addition to a medical background, management and legal skills are important. Professional administrators are business managers first. They must implement procedures that ensure the entity will be profitable so that it can continue to exist.

An administrator with legal training has an advantage in managing a health care organization because of the interplay between insurance coverage and treatment choices and the potential liability of the organization in the event that the treatment is not successful. In addition, the administrator must understand employee relations issues, including labor law and benefits, and be adept at fundraising and community relations. While all large organizations will employ specialists in each area, the leader must understand the various functions of the organization to provide informed leadership.

A health care organization will likely be managed like a for-profit corporation, though it will be incorporated as a nonprofit organization. The same departments and functions discussed in Chapter 7 should apply to health care organizations.

Engineering and Architectural Firms

Legal training can be beneficial to engineering and architectural firms handling government contracts. In addition to an understanding of the pertinent engineering and architectural concepts, an understanding of government contract compliance regulations and reporting requirements is essential for a position as a contract administrator. Although engineering and architectural experience is more important than legal experience for most positions in this area, legal training can be an asset when performing general administrative duties.

Large engineering and architectural companies have personnel departments, plus many of the other departments discussed in the Corporations and Their Departments section of Chapter 7. With a little creativity and a background in engineering or architecture, legal training can aid in finding a job in the industry.

Environmental and Land Use Management Firms

Hazardous waste clean-up and disposal, as well as environmental disaster clean-up, require an understanding of the science involved in returning the environment to its natural state. Environmental and land use management firms employ engineers and environmental scientists to handle the technical work of the firm. Similar to the engineering firms discussed above, an understanding of government regulations and contract administration is essential. For the firm to be successful, it must be able to submit acceptable bids to the governmental entity that is soliciting the services of an environmental firm. Submitting a winning bid that allows the company to complete the project and make a profit requires an understanding of the complexity of the project and the costs involved with performing the work requested. This requires a combination of legal skills, management-budgeting skills, and a scientific under-standing of the environmental work to be done.

Counseling Firms

Still another field where lawyers frequently create their own busi-nesses is in the area of counseling, mediation, and arbitration. Such lawyers frequently have training in counseling or a related discipline, in addition to law. With the rise in interest in alternative dispute resolution, it is an area where growth can be expected in the coming years. Several law schools now offer degrees in alter-native dispute resolution. Those schools should be able to help with alumni placement.

▼▼▼▼▼

Paul had practiced law for twenty years before he decided he needed a lifestyle change. He had worked in a large law firm during his first ten years of practice and then left with some of the other partners to form a small law firm. When the small law firm grew into a large law firm, Paul decided that he no longer needed the pressure. Paul left the firm and traveled for a year. At the end of his sabbatical, he decided to become a mediator. He opened his own mediation service and took referrals from his friends in practice. He enjoys the slower pace of his practice and he still makes a comfortable living. Although he does not have a degree in dispute resolution, he recommends that anyone inter-ested to start in this field take as many classes as possible and earn a dispute-resolution degree.

Investigation Firms

A number of lawyers work as private investigators. They may have backgrounds in military intelligence, the FBI (many of whose agents are lawyers), military intelligence, or some other law enforcement agency. Lawyer-investigators frequently enjoy solving the puzzles more than taking the cases to court, yet everything they do involves some aspect of the law and legal relationships. Investigation firms often work closely with law firms on both plaintiff and defendant sides.

▼▼▼▼▼

Nick had been a police officer before law school, but figured that he could make a lot more money practicing law. When he graduated, he got a job with the district attorney, putting away the people he had arrested before. But Nick was never satisfied with the routine of legal work; even trials were more drudgery and less excitement than he had anticipated. He longed for the challenge of putting the pieces of a case together as he had done in police work. At the suggestion of someone in his office, he decided to explore the possibilities of private investigation and shortly thereafter decided to take the plunge. The contacts he had made as a lawyer kept his business thriving, and his lawyering skills enhanced his investigative skills. In the end, Nick found everything he wanted in a career and made a decent living as well.

Personal Financial Services

No listing of professional services would be complete without mentioning personal financial services. In past generations, this category was primarily dominated by life insurance sales and stock brokerage. One typically had an insurance agent and a stockbroker, both of whom were associated with a major insurance carrier or brokerage house. Since the 1980s, however, the investment picture has become increasingly complex. Independent agents who sell a number of financial products compete with company agents who continue to maintain a relationship with a particular company. The number and type of investment opportunities has increased, and the financial sales people today typically offer a range of products to consumers. On top of this, the financial planning industry, which focuses first on long-term financial growth and secondarily on acquisition of particular products to meet those needs, has grown dramatically. One may now become a certified financial planner, as well as an agent for certain financial products or institutions. A partial listing of the activities that fall within this general category follows:

- General financial planning
- Retirement planning
- Financial crisis planning
- Stock brokerage
- Mutual fund sales
- Bond sales
- Other creative investments
- Insurance sales

Lawyers have in the past pursued careers in the personal financial services industry, in part because their knowledge of the legal aspects of complex contracts such as insurance policies, initial public offerings (IPOs), and similar instruments can serve clients well, but also because the bonus structure for sales positions can be quite lucrative. Although many lawyers may be uncomfortable in the sales arena, some may find it challenging and rewarding.

Multiprofessional Firms

As society has grown more complex, so have the types of professional services firms that aim to help individuals and organizations resolve problems. In many countries the roles of lawyers and nonlawyers are increasingly becoming amalgamated into large "one-stop-shopping" professional services organizations. These multiprofessional firms practices have generated considerable controversy in the United States, when the American Bar Association declined to amend ethics rules prohibiting partnerships and fee sharing with nonlawyers.

Combined Professional Services

In 2000, the ABA voted to retain existing ethics rules prohibiting lawyers from forming partnerships or sharing fees with nonlawyers. See ABA Model Rules of Professional Conduct, Rule 5.4. Notwithstanding this limitation, however, many legal and nonlegal professional service providers are experimenting with creative, informal service delivery systems that accomplish multidisciplinary service without violating the rules of ethics. An increasing number of clients are demanding multiprofessional approaches to problem solving, and in fact many legal problems are inherently multiprofessional in terms of the services required to resolve them. Thus, each year more lawyers move from the traditional practice of law to some form of nonlegal service that involves a team of professionals to serve clients with complex problems.

Law Firm Ancillary Businesses

Although law firms cannot have law firm partners, in most states they are permitted to own ancillary or subsidiary businesses (see ABA Model Rules of Professional Conduct, Rule 5.7). Despite restrictions governing such organizations, law firms can develop consulting, software, market analysis, litigation support, and a variety of other law-related companies, which serve the law firm, but also sell law-related services on the open market.

These so-called ancillary businesses pose conflicts and other problems and have not grown dramatically. Some firms have even sold or spun off their ancillary businesses, because they were too difficult to manage. For purposes of this book, it is worth recognizing that such organizations do exist, and that they represent one avenue for transition from law practice to nonlegal work.

▼▼▼▼▼

John was a litigation partner with a major American law firm and, over the years, an innovator in the field of litigation support technology. He oversaw the development of one of the most sophisticated litigation support departments in the United States, while maintaining a full caseload at the firm. Eventually, Charles persuaded the firm to create a subsidiary company, which would continue to serve the firm but would also sell computer animations and case management software to other firms. Charles and his firm held all the stock in the new company, and Charles became its CEO. Charles then phased out his litigation practice to concentrate on running the company. Still later, the firm decided to sell its interest in the litigation support company to Charles and other investors. The firm still uses Charles's company for its litigation support.

Dual Professionals

One other category of work deserves mention, because it crosses over from legal to nonlegal work: lawyers who engage in dual professions. The most common of these dual professional arrangements are law and medicine, law and accounting, and law and science or engineering. These dual-profession lawyers practice law and another profession at the same time. Although there are ethical pitfalls to avoid, a dual profession may be an ideal way for some people to maintain their links to law practice while engaging in entrepreneurial activity outside the law.

Although the foregoing categories include activities where legally trained individuals frequently work, the list is not intended to be exhaustive. Lawyer-entrepreneurs can engage in any kind of business activity they choose. They may or may not get involved in such activity through their clients. Their legal expertise may or may not be critical to their success in the business. Their nonlegal skills may or may not be necessary prerequisites. Creative entrepreneurial ventures that meet people's needs to resolve their legal problems in efficient and economical ways will succeed, regardless of whether they are provided within the traditional legal profession or judicial system.

Publishing and Media   **11**

The expanding world of media is no longer limited to newspapers, magazines, books, radio, and television. Today the Internet has radically changed the way media companies deliver their products. Publishing, cable television, pay-per-view television, satellite television, movies, music, radio, and music videos are being delivered to consumers in a variety of modes. Personal computers and the Internet have forced traditional media companies to expand their delivery systems and to continue to explore new technology. With these technological advances has come the need for people who understand the legal implications of their applications.

The discussion in Chapter 7 concerning the various departments in a corporation applies to media conglomerates. Media companies are some of the largest international corporations in America. Filmed entertainment is the largest American export. It is a creative business that may require some perseverance and individual imagination to infiltrate.

Most larger media companies have an internal business affairs division in addition to a legal department.

Members of this department negotiate the deals for the acquisition of talent and creative products, such as manuscripts, scripts, screenplays, music, and completed movies or television programs. Both lawyers and nonlawyers hold these positions, but those with legal training are filling the new positions and have a better chance for advancement as they develop their expertise. After a deal has been negotiated, the lawyers in the legal department translate the deal into legalese. For detailed information on the job possibilities in the entertainment industry, read the ABA Career Series publication *Entertainment Law Careers* by William D. Henslee (ABA, 1998).

Media positions at all levels of administration are being filled by individuals with law degrees. The presidents of some of the major studios were at one time practicing lawyers. Legal training is considered a strong background credential for many positions.

There are many reporters and news anchors who attended law school. Geraldo Rivera, Catherine Crier, and many other lawyers host television and radio shows, serve as commentators, and even—like David E. Kelly—produce television shows and films. If you have the talent and the inclination, pursue your dreams. It is not easy to break into a media position, but the right job can be worth the persistence and effort.

Editors

Editors are professional readers, much like transactional lawyers. The skills developed in proofreading legal documents easily translate into reading articles and books. Attention to detail is an essential skill for an editor. The ability to understand the text and suggest additions or deletions to clarify the message or make the story more compelling is a skill that is shared by lawyers and editors.

All of the largest publishing houses are headquartered in New York City. The legal publishing houses are not concentrated in New York, but there are very few of them. On a local level, newspapers employ editors. Newspaper editors are usually journalists who have worked their way up from reporter to editor. Editors are managers who have a background in journalism and have paid their

dues at the company. Writing for a publication may be
in a long-term strategy if your goal is to become an edi
Publishers section below for more information on publi.

▼▼▼▼▼

Heather was an English major in college and went to law school
because she thought it would help her get a job. There weren't
many jobs for English majors when she graduated from college.
Heather loved writing and wanted to do something with her
background that did not entail writing legal briefs for a law firm.
She didn't have a position when she graduated from law school
because she hadn't looked very hard. After consulting with her
career planning office, she got the names of local publishing
companies and sent in her résumé. Because of her legal background, several publishing companies were interested in talking
to her. Heather finally decided to take a position as an editor at a
local legal press. She enjoyed the regular hours and the fact that
she could combine her undergraduate training with her legal
training. She is not sure where she is going to go from her current job, but she is comfortable and happy with her choice to
become an editor rather than a practicing lawyer.

Writers

Writers, reporters, researchers, and analysts represent another
group of lawyer-entrepreneurs. Such individuals may work for
other organizations (such as a newspaper), or they may also start
their own businesses or operate independently on a freelance
basis. Lawyers who have practiced for a few years find that truth
is stranger than fiction—if the lawyer is so inclined, the experiences of the past can become the material for a future as a writer.
Don't quit your day job unless you have sold at least two of your
works for a substantial sum of money. You want to make sure that
the first sale was not a fluke.

The joke that every lawyer in Los Angeles has written a script
is closer to the truth than you might imagine. Remember to avoid
claims of defamation by making your characters fictitious. Issues

of privacy and publicity should be considered when writing about your experiences. The real-life characters may not like the way their on-screen characters are portrayed if you present them in a negative or embarrassing light. If you are inclined to turn your experiences into a script, make sure you investigate the proper format for script submissions. There is a science to the art. Like the courts' strict requirements for submission of documents, Hollywood has similar rules. Amateurs who submit their material in an improper format give the readers one more reason to reject the script. There are several software programs that will do the formatting for you if you are interested in writing a script.

Novels have made John Grisham and Scott Turow household names. Their work has been adapted into films and has inspired a genre of television programs. The great thing about writing is that it can be done without quitting your regular job. Dedicate one to two hours a day, preferably at the same time each day, for writing. Keep in mind, though that writing is a long and solitary process, so it is not for everyone.

Writing magazine and newspaper articles in your area of expertise is a way to become known as a writer and to earn a little extra money. If you are thinking of transitioning into a new practice area, or a new, nonlegal industry, writing articles on timely issues in the field is an excellent way to introduce yourself to your new constituents and colleagues.

Radio and Television

Radio and television present opportunities for lawyers as on-air talent and as executives. Legal correspondents are regulars on national and local news programs. If your local television news station does not have a regular legal news segment, you may have an opportunity to become that correspondent. Political analysts are employed around election time and crime analysts are on every news channel when a major trial is underway. To secure one of these on-air positions, you must be either an expert on the topic or a natural on-air talent. A pleasant yet distinctive speaking voice and a television-friendly face are necessary for television. You only need the voice for radio.

If acting is your passion, you will need to head to Hollywood to get cast in a television show. It is unusual, but not unheard of, for lawyers to become actors. Senator Fred Thompson retired from the United States Senate to become a full-time actor on the *Law and Order* programs. A caveat is in order: legal training will not substitute for acting ability. Courtroom training, however, may help prepare you for an acting career.

Television is a writer's medium. Writers drive the productions and often serve as the executive producers of the programs. Writers with legal training are employed by producers as members of the writing team, or as consultants, on the many courtroom dramas on television. A background as a prosecutor or public defender is generally a prerequisite for a position with a courtroom drama. (Doctors are employed in the same manner for the medical dramas.)

Lawyers are employed in all facets of radio and television management. The corporate structure of the stations was discussed above. In addition to the traditional legal positions, lawyers are television producers. David E. Kelly is a former lawyer who is now a very successful producer.

▼▼▼▼▼

Glenn did not want to practice law when he graduated from law school in Los Angeles. Following graduation, he searched the trade publications *Variety* and *The Hollywood Reporter,* for jobs for which he might be qualified. Prior to law school, he had worked for a boxing promoter as a media salesman. When he saw a job listed by a major studio for a position as a television sales representative, he applied and was hired. He was sent to the Midwest to cover television stations in a five-state area. Glenn visited independent stations to sell the studio's syndicated programs. He lived on the road even though he had an apartment in Chicago. After two years on the road, he started looking for another position in the company. When a business affairs position opened up in Los Angeles, he applied and was accepted. He moved back to Los Angeles into a quasi-legal position. Glenn enjoyed using his legal training while he negotiated contracts with producers and talent agents.

Film

Film has similar opportunities for lawyers as television. Film studios are corporations with traditional corporate structures. Depending on the size of the studio, the corporate cultures range from button-down corporate to blue-jeans casual. All of the possibilities that exist in television and writing discussed above also exist in film.

An individual film production is like a small corporation that is organized for a single project. The company may employ hundreds of employees, including grips, teamsters, set designers, make-up artists, costume designers, carpenters, electricians, actors, directors, writers, camera operators, editors, location scouts, caterers, security guards, and production assistants. The producer is like the president of the company. Once the production is complete, the company is disbanded and all of the employees are released for their next projects. Producers who are lawyers are trained to handle the enormous amount of paperwork involved with every production.

▼▼▼▼▼

Bridgette went to law school after earning her undergraduate degree from film school. Following law school, she used her connections to get an entry-level position in the business affairs department of an independent production company. When she joined the company, her boss was a lawyer who needed help because of the company's expansion. As one of only two lawyers in the company, Bridgette was able to move up quickly by taking on more responsibility. Within a year of joining the company, she was named a vice president. She was able to hire a friend from law school to help in the department. Bridgette's legal education helped her understand the importance of certain deal points, and helped her understand the legal terms of art that are used in the industry to cover those points. She is now the president of the company.

▼▼▼▼▼

Brent graduated from law school and went to work in the mailroom of a major talent agency. After a year in the mailroom, he was promoted to assistant. As an assistant, he worked for the head of the feature film department. Assistants listen to all of the telephone calls made by their bosses. Brent was a quick study and learned how to structure talent and literary rights deals by listening and reading everything that passed across his desk. After six months as an assistant, Brent left the agency to work in the business-affairs department of an independent production company. Since leaving the agency, Brent has been promoted twice, from the head of business affairs to the head of creative affairs. As a vice president of creative affairs, Brent reads scripts instead of contracts. He loves his work, but he does not plan on staying in his position too long. His next goal is to produce films. Brent's law degree helped put his career on a fast track.

Publishers

By the end of law school most students are aware of the existence of legal publishers, even though the tasks that lawyers perform within these organizations may be unclear. There are, as in most other nonlegal job settings, a variety of administrative opportunities. The editorial function is performed by legally trained editors.

In addition to the legal press, opportunities exist throughout the general publishing business. Every hardcover book, paperback book, magazine, and newspaper has a publisher. In addition, there are publishers for schoolbooks, encyclopedias, specialty books, and periodicals on virtually every conceivable subject. Each of these publishers employs editorial staff members, who usually have a specialized background in the subject peculiar to the publication. There are those involved in the administration of the total enterprise, as well as individuals who perform the specialized activities of the publishing world.

▼▼▼▼▼

Patrice got a job as a low-level editor at a major publishing house immediately upon graduation from college. She moved quickly up the ranks, taking on a series of increasingly responsible and challenging jobs. Eventually, she had responsibility for worldwide production of titles for her company. Then the company was taken over by an even larger publishing conglomerate, and Patrice decided to go to law school as a kind of career insurance. She kept her day job, and went to law school at night, thriving in both environments. She survived her company's consolidation and graduated at the top of her law school class. She found, however, that her salary as a senior executive in the publishing firm was more than she could expect to earn in even the largest law firm, so Patrice continues to work at the same job, while contemplating either a move to the legal department within the company or a postretirement legal career. And she still has her law degree in case things change at work.

Literary agents negotiate with the publishing company on behalf of authors. Legal training has not traditionally been a prerequisite for agents; however, there are a few agents with legal training and there are opportunities for industrious lawyers. Should you be interested in a position as an agent in the entertainment industry, read the ABA Career Series book *Entertainment Law Careers* by William D. Henslee (ABA, 1998).

Westlaw and LexisNexis employ law school graduates as editors, case reviewers for head note designations, salespersons, and administrators. Positions are available in both the hardback book divisions and the computer-assisted research divisions. The other legal press companies employ law school graduates in similar positions.

Regardless of your background, you will have to start at the bottom like everyone else in the industry, unless you possess prelegal experience in the field. Once you become established, however, your background and credentials will help you advance.

Educational Institutions

12

General Considerations

Educational institutions use lawyers and individuals with legal training in all aspects of the organization. Every university has a general counsel, but that is an in-house legal position rather than a nonlegal position. This chapter focuses on the many other positions that lawyers fill in educational institutions as all levels, including both teachers and administrators.

Educational institutions come in all manner of shapes and sizes, and include both privately and publicly funded institutions. It would be impossible to describe the multitude of positions in these institutions, and misleading to generalize. If you are thinking about a career in education, the best way to get a feel for the positions that are available is to read the *Chronicle of Higher Education* or the *New York Times* Education Section listings for job openings. Many academic disciplines also publish newsletters and online listings of positions.

This chapter is divided into three sections: Elementary and Secondary Education, Postsecondary and Graduate Education, and Legal Education. Within each of these broad categories, positions can be divided between teaching and administrative work, though it is not uncommon for individuals to do both, sometimes at the same time and sometimes at different times in their careers.

Special teaching credentials may be required for some posts, but teaching positions at all levels are open to lawyers. With an advanced degree, you begin at a higher pay level in most public school systems. The higher the educational level (elementary, secondary, college, graduate school, and law school), the more important the individual's academic credentials are for consideration for the position. Colleges and law schools require advanced degrees, publications, and work experience.

In the case of administration, lawyers may be found at all levels of academic institutions. The presidents of several universities are lawyers, as well as other high-ranking administrators. Lawyers may occupy any administrative position if they bring other relevant experience to the job. Fundraising for major gifts and planned giving are essential activities in many organizations. These posi-

▼▼▼▼▼

Emilio enjoyed working in the law library while in law school and decided to pursue a career as a law librarian. After graduation from law school, Emilio worked in his law school library full time. To advance in the profession, and become the director of a law library, Emilio's boss told him that he would have to return to school to earn a master's of library science. He found a part-time program that allowed him to continue to work in the library and attend classes at night. After he finished his MLS degree, Emilio started looking for advancement. After serving as an associate director for two years, he found a directorship position. After three years as the director, Emilio was promoted to an associate deanship. He teaches at the law school and is working on receiving tenure by publishing in his field. Emilio enjoys the managerial responsibility of running a law library and teaching. He has found his perfect position.

tions are increasingly being filled by individuals with legal training. (For a brief explanation of fundraising, see the discussion in the section "Foundations and Charitable Organizations" in Chapter 9.)

Librarianship is an option for law school graduates seeking a career that combines academics with management skills. A master's of library science (MLS) or a master's of information and library science (MILS) degree is required as an additional academic credential necessary for advancement in the profession. For further information on a career as a law librarian, consult the library director at your law school, or contact the American Association of Law Libraries, which is based in Chicago.

Primary and Secondary Education

Although the number of lawyers who work as teachers and administrators in public and private schools in the grades K–12 (generally referred to as primary and secondary education) is small, it is by no means negligible. For many lawyers who just want to teach, but do not find opportunities at the college and university level, teaching high school or even grade school may represent a feasible alternative. Bar passage will usually not be sufficient for licensure (although it may help in boost the salary level because schools tend to give credit for advanced degrees), so prospective teachers will need to seek a teaching certificate, which may involve going back to school to obtain the necessary credentials.

Postsecondary and Graduate Education

Lawyers interested in education may want to explore postsecondary and graduate education (the college and university level), including liberal arts and specialized four-year colleges, publicly and privately funded universities, and two-year community colleges. Depending on the field, opportunities may be as competitive for faculty positions as law school faculty positions, and, with the exception of a department looking specifically for a lawyer (e.g., a business school looking for someone to teach business law), candidates will have to possess sterling credentials in the academic field they seek to enter. Many law students who did graduate work before coming to law school may have competitive credentials, but others may need to go back to school to enhance their credentials before applying. Some of the subject areas where lawyers may have particular qualifications include:

- Business law
- Labor relations
- Business regulation
- Equal employment
- Business ethics
- Biomedical ethics
- Legal history
- Jurisprudence
- Philosophy of law
- Law as applied to a substantive field (e.g., engineering)

Some law graduates may want to pursue administrative positions instead of teaching positions, as described in the "Legal Education" section below; not surprisingly, positions outside the law school are analogous to those in legal education, but relatively more numerous.

It is worth noting that community colleges continue to grow nationally, whereas institutions offering four-year and graduate degrees have stabilized. It is also the case that many faculty positions at two-year colleges and some lower-end four-year institutions are for adjunct (part-time) teachers and do not pay well enough to support someone on a full-time basis.

Legal Education

One of the areas where the growth of opportunities for legally trained individuals over the course of the last two decades has been most noticeable is in the field of legal education. Although law schools have always been comprised of a dean and faculty, the tendency to hire lawyers for other administrative positions in the law school has been nothing less than dramatic. A recent informal survey suggests that as many as 80 percent of the senior non-teaching administrators in law schools today are lawyers. Some of the areas where these individuals work include the following:

- Career services
- Financial aid
- Admissions
- Admissions recruiting
- Student services
- Academic support and counseling
- Business affairs
- Continuing legal education
- External affairs
- Fundraising and development
- Alumni affairs
- Registrar
- Human resources and benefits
- Program and center directors
- Legal research
- Information technology
- Law librarians (without faculty appointment)

Some of these individuals may be graduates of the law school where they work, and others are expatriates of the world of law practice. They are attracted by the civil atmosphere and relatively low pressure of academic institutions, as well as the intellectually stimulating work setting. To put this into perspective, if there are approximately 200 law schools in the United States with an average of twenty nonfaculty administrative positions, and lawyers hold 80 percent of the slots, this represents approximately 3,200 jobs. Of course, these figures are estimates, but it gives you some idea of the numbers.

Lifetime and Continuing Education

The field of lifetime, continuing and adult education is another growing field. The aging baby boomers, who will be retiring in large numbers between now and 2025, will seek advanced education in a variety of settings: residential university programs, elder hostels, travel and learning programs, and online education. Many of the topics that will interest them will have legal overtones as they seek to manage their retirement funds, lifestyles and health management, and for this reason lawyers will be in demand as these opportunities grow.

Academic Research

A final category of work in periphery of education is academic research. Many institutions of higher learning seek funding for a variety of academic research projects. Some of these projects are supported by ongoing centers, while others are connected to academic departments or individual professors. In some cases, the research facility or think tank may include a public purpose, and funding may come not only from grants, but also from public funds. For lawyers who have highly specialized backgrounds and research skills, this may be an area worth pursuing.

Information and *Technology* 13

Another broad area of entrepreneurial activity for lawyers is in the area of computers and information technology. Again, such individuals must possess special skills in the technological field, though law may prove valuable in a number of ways. Certainly, technological support to legal practitioners is an important component of this field, but lawyer "techies" can be found in a number of nonlegal businesses as well.

Information Technology Specialists

Although we do not usually think of lawyers as information technology specialists, a subset of every law school class possesses a high level of technological expertise. These skills can be used in a legal environment, but they are relevant to other fields as well. In addition, legal training may give the IT specialist unique knowledge in working with information systems.

Technology Consultants

As with IT specialists, technology consultants work with companies and firms to provide contractual tech support. Although law firm support is a unique niche in this market, the same kind of work is carried on in virtually every industry, and for small companies that cannot support in-house IT consultants provide the technical support needed to keep those organizations running.

▼▼▼▼▼

Jan had worked as a law librarian for several years following law school. Her last three years in the profession were spent as the director of a law school library. As a student of new technology, Jan loved to work with the latest equipment and software. She found that her law school could not stay on the cutting edge of technology because of the high cost of changing the massive systems. Jan decided to leave the school and become an IT consultant so that she could help law firms and schools keep up with changing technologies. She was able to use her student connections to get introductions to law firms, corporations, and government officials. She studied the bid process, learned the politics of presentations, and won several large consulting jobs. She loves the freedom of working for herself and the opportunity to use the latest technology as she upgrades systems for her clients.

Web Site Design

In the world of the Internet, the growth of company Web sites has continued unabated. Although the growth of this business has slowed as most companies and firms have gained an Internet presence, new startup companies need support, as well as companies with antiquated or ineffective Web sites. This is particularly true in the legal arena, where law firms are generally behind the business curve in creating sophisticated Internet services.

Litigation Support and Document Management

Continuing to look at the legal environment, it is worth noting that litigation and document management have continued to spawn new and innovative services to support the work of lawyers that in some ways had not changed in hundreds of years. The movement of courts to accept electronic filing, discovery, hearings, computer animations, and evidence has pushed trial lawyers in the direction of litigation support services. Whether the services are represented by software, hardware, Internet applications, or consulting services, this burgeoning industry is still in its infancy. Lawyers with technology backgrounds will find a variety of opportunities here.

Graphics and Animation

Whereas accidents used to be depicted by charts displayed on an easel, lawyers now use increasingly sophisticated animations and computer graphics to display demonstrative evidence in charts, recreations, graphic messages, and sound. This is an area where George Lucas seems to meet Clarence Darrow, where Madison Avenue meets the Inns of Court, and where the future holds a promise of continued growth.

Information and Knowledge Management

The last field to mention in this litany of technology is information and knowledge management (KM). At one time, this area was known as database management, but the focus on databases failed to do justice to the promise of the technology. Knowledge management is the leverage of information within an organization or population to maximize its usefulness to the organization. Although KM raises a number of issues—including privacy and for lawyers conflicts of interest—the potential to serve lawyers and the public is tremendous.

The speculative nature of the opportunities in the technology field merely illustrate how volatile and evolutionary it is. The authors include these emerging fields not only because they represent real options for real lawyers today, but they also represent the challenge of forecasting the appearance of new opportunities in the future.

Entrepreneurial Ventures **14**

A surprisingly large number of lawyers are entrepreneurs—that is, people who start and run their own individual businesses. Although sole proprietors and operators of small businesses are sometimes called entrepreneurs, true entrepreneurs create a business, and many continue to run their "brain children" throughout their lives. According to this definition, many practicing lawyers qualify as entrepreneurs, including the law school graduate who hangs out a shingle, the group of senior associates who split off from an existing firm, and the retired government lawyer who opens up a practice at the age of sixty-five. Many of the general statements that can be made about entrepreneurs apply to entrepreneurial lawyers as well.

This chapter, however, focuses primarily on lawyers who engage in entrepreneurial activities outside of private practice. Some of these ventures are law-related, in which lawyers provide specialized services to other lawyers and law firms on a contract basis. As the legal profession has grown more complex, and small boutique firms have become more prominent in the marketplace, cottage industries have appeared to support the work of organizations that do not have in-house staff to handle certain activities. For example, a large firm may have a management information systems (MIS) director responsible for computer systems as a full-time employee. A small firm would more likely hire a consultant on an as-needed basis to provide systems support. The consultant might not necessarily be a lawyer, though legal training is a valuable asset in addressing the technology needs of legal clients. In fact, an increasing number of technology consultants in the law are themselves lawyers.

Not everyone is cut out to be an entrepreneur. For many people, the security of a monthly paycheck is more appealing than the thought of an income dependent on the unpredictable fluctuations of the business cycle. For some, the stability of working in an organization where systems are in place is more attractive than the uncertainty and chaos associated with creating systems out of nothing at all. Some people enjoy taking ongoing projects to a conclusion more than starting new ones. Certain people feel more comfortable in an organization with many coworkers than working alone or with a very small group of people.

On the other hand, some people thrive on the independence, risk, creative energy, and uncertainty of genesis. Research shows that entrepreneurs have a very high need for autonomy and an aversion to hierarchy. They are not risk-averse, but rather derive satisfaction from taking chances and succeeding. They tend to have strong organizational skills, at least in their ability to actualize abstract concepts.

There is also some evidence to suggest that many successful entrepreneurs come from a family tradition of entrepreneurial activity or else benefited from entrepreneur role models during their formative years. Such individuals may gain an assurance that it is possible to succeed in a startup enterprise, and they may also learn specific skills that help them to succeed in such an environment.

Financial considerations can influence the decision to start a business from scratch as well. A person who leads a Spartan lifestyle and has few financial commitments to a family, student loans, or investments may be in a better position to start a business than someone with a heavy debt load or numerous obligations. For couples, the decision for one or both to engage in entrepreneurial activities requires that both be absolutely committed to that goal. It may help to have access to funds—savings, retirement, a family trust fund, or a working spouse—not only for living expenses, but also for startup capital. Many successful business people, however, start out with literally nothing and build a business from the ground up.

It is no secret that the failure rate for new businesses is extremely high. Although the percentages vary from industry to industry, every entrepreneur must accept the risk of failure. Many successful entrepreneurs testify to having undertaken several businesses that failed before hitting on a formula that worked. If you grew up in the economic stability of the 1970s or 1980s, the thought of business failure may be intimidating; perhaps starting a new business is just not for you. If you need a safety net or a guarantee that you will succeed, you should probably not consider it.

Some people become entrepreneurs out of necessity rather than design. They either do not find a job when they graduate from law school, get fired or laid off, or find themselves in an unrewarding dead-end position. For some, the possibility of starvation or stagnation teaches them that they have skills they were not aware of. These people learn that necessity is truly the mother of invention.

Whether they plan it or not, an increasing number of lawyers will become entrepreneurs in the future. In some areas, the market for lawyers is simply saturated. There are just not enough jobs practicing law for the number of lawyers qualified to do so.

Although fluctuations in the business cycle dictate that certain periods provide a better business climate than others, the problems brought on by the growth of the legal profession transcend the short-term effects of recession and recovery. In other words, regardless of the state of the economy, legally trained individuals will face intense competition for traditional jobs in the coming decade.

Furthermore, changes in society as a whole, precipitated by developments in the electronic media and other new forms of technology, are transforming the way people work. The benefits of large corporate structures are no longer appealing, compared to smaller organizations that can be operated out of the home, the office, or even the car. These changes give entrepreneurial activities an edge in flexibility and responsiveness to the needs of a complex business environment and favor the entrepreneurial lawyer. Such changes generate a host of new opportunities for those with the necessary vision and fortitude.

The process of starting a business involves several distinct phases:

- Conceptualization—In cartoons, this is the light bulb over a character's head—the germ of an idea. Although almost everyone has ideas from time to time, not everyone can make those ideas come to life. Thus, conceptualization also includes thinking through a plan in detail.

- Planning—This is committing to paper the specifics of the plan in a form that can be communicated to others. A document known as a business plan is often the embodiment of this process. In some cases, the first two phases are merged into one, and in other cases verbal communication supplants a written document; in some instances, the entrepreneur may "just do it."

- Financing—Almost all businesses require at least some capitalization, whether it comes from the entrepreneur's savings, a bank loan, or a stock offering. Professional services businesses like law do not require the same kind of capital investment as an industrial concern needing specialized machinery or a retail business requiring an up-front investment in inventory. At a minimum, you will probably need at least a computer and a fax machine and enough cash for office supplies and operations. You will need enough money for living expenses to cover your first year of operation, because chances are you will not take anything out of your business until the second year. If you have to go to others for financing, the business plan will be critical in this effort.

- Startup—This is putting all the pieces together—letting people know that you are ready to serve them, and opening your doors to clients. This phase is probably the most crucial to the way you are perceived by your future clients, because first impressions are often lasting ones. Countless details, deadlines, and last-minute glitches undoubtedly make this period a stressful one for the entrepreneur.

- Implementation—This involves getting the business off the ground once its doors are opened. This phase inevitably involves fine tuning, or working out the kinks.

- Transition—The last phase is a transition to an ongoing operation—after systems and methods of operation are in place, the bugs are worked out, and a positive cash flow is generated.

One of the most difficult parts of the entire process for many individuals, particularly those who lack formal business training, is the creation of a business plan. The business plan should contain several basic elements:

- Statement of the concept—You should be able to clearly articulate a paragraph or two about what your business will do, for whom it will do it, and how its goals will be accomplished. If you cannot succinctly articulate an overview, it will be almost impossible for you to complete the document or to sell the idea to anyone else.

- Market analysis—The market analysis should assess the need for the product or service you propose to deliver. This should include information about the demographics of your target audience, proof to support your assertion that your product or service is needed, and surveys to show that your audience will buy. The market analysis also should evaluate actual and potential competitors—businesses that target the same audience and provide the same product or service that you do. The analysis should identify a market niche. A niche is the segment of the market that you will stake out as yours, because no one else is meeting that particular need, or because you believe you can service that need better, faster, and cheaper than your competitors. The market analysis should conclude with a definite plan for articulating your availability to the target audience; in other words, how people will find out about you.

- Organizational analysis—This should include a statement of who will be working for you and what they will do. If the business is just you, an analysis should indicate that you possess the skills to do the tasks that need to be done. If you propose to contract for certain services such as legal counsel, accounting, bookkeeping, secretarial services, or other activities that you cannot perform yourself, the analysis should state specifically who you will use and what the service will cost. If you have an ongoing relationship with a bank or other lender, you should disclose it. The organizational analysis also should project how your staffing needs will change as the organization grows. For instance, you may not plan to hire a secretary until after the first year of operation. You may foresee that your organization of one person will grow to twenty or more.

◆ Financial analysis—This should incorporate a *pro forma* budget, covering at least two years of projected income and expenses. In addition, a cash-flow analysis should demonstrate that bills will be paid during the startup phases of the business. A statement of assets and liabilities for the business, as well as for you personally, should be included. If you contemplate securing a loan, credit references are a necessity. The assistance of a CPA can be invaluable in formulating the financial analysis for your business. Because any lender or investor will take a hard look at your figures, it is critical that they be accurate and realistic.

What do lawyer entrepreneurs do? The simple answer is that lawyers get involved in just about every kind of business you can imagine. The following descriptions, however, cover a number of the common areas, although these are only a few examples of the many possibilities. For more information, see *The Lawyer's Guide to Creating a Business Plan: A Step-by-Step Software Package,* by Linda Pinson (ABA, 2006).

Consultants

A growing segment of the business world is consulting work. Although one may consult about anything, and pundits sometimes suggest that consultants are professionals without jobs, the truth is that many businesses see the benefit of purchasing expertise on the open market rather than employing individuals in-house. One reason for this might be that the company does not have enough work to hire a full-time employee. Another reason might be that the business needs an impartial outside opinion.

Some organizations use independent contractor consultants to limit their liability because an independent contractor is less likely to subject a business concern to vicarious liability than is an employee acting within the scope of his employment. Some companies may use consulting services because the individual they want does not seek or require a full-time job, but prefers an alternative work arrangement.

Lawyer consultants fall into two major groups: those who provide law-related services, as opposed to legal representation, to nonlegal entities, and those who provide nonlegal support services to other lawyers.

Agents

A second group of entrepreneurs who are lawyers include the broad classification of agents. Agents may work for sports or entertainment figures, individual or family business interests, trusts, or even businesses. For more information on a career as a sports agent read the ABA Career Series publication *Careers in Sports Law* by Kenneth L. Shropshire (ABA, 1990). William D. Henslee's *Entertainment Law Careers* (ABA, 1998) includes information on agents in the entertainment field. A lawyer who represents the business interests of others as an agent may use her legal expertise, but the representation is not a traditional lawyer-client relationship.

To actively pursue clients as most successful agents must, you may decide to resign from the bar so as not to subject yourself to discipline for violation of your state's professional conduct rules. If you are a lawyer, you are not allowed to violate your state's professional conduct rules while you are acting as an agent. You do not get to decide when you are a lawyer and when you are an agent; as a member of the bar, you are always a lawyer.

Several states impose registration requirements for agents. Some states exempt lawyers from those requirements. Before you decide to become an agent, check with your particular state to find out if you must register before you can work as an agent. All of the professional sports have agent registration requirements that are separate from the state requirements.

Venture Capitalists

Venture capitalists fund startup companies for either a debt or equity position and one or more seats on the board of directors. If you are independently wealthy, or you represent a number of clients who are independently wealthy, you may consider organizing a venture capital group. The fund administrator is either a salaried employee of the group or an independent contractor who takes a percentage of the amount invested.

Knowledge of SEC regulations and the rules pertaining to qualified and unqualified investors are required to work in this area. Knowing people with a large amount of disposable income is also critical.

Startup Specialists

Startup specialists help entrepreneurs incorporate and find startup funding. Like the work of an agent, startup specialists work on the border between legal and nonlegal work. The work of corporate formation may be more on the legal side, but securing capital or other financing, helping to structure the business, and even advising on startup management involves a variety of nonlegal skills as well.

Conclusion | **15**

This book does not include all potential job settings for legally trained individuals. Our goal is to get you thinking creatively about the possibilities that exist for someone with your training and background. With the knowledge and work ethic you have established, you should be able to create a position that suits your talents.

The overall picture of the legal profession is one of a large group of highly educated and intelligent individuals serving society in a wide variety of settings. Although the most prominent segment of the lawyer population engages in the private practice of law, followed by other traditional forms of practice, many legally trained people engage in activities beyond the scope of traditional legal representation. Many of these activities incorporate legal elements, and almost all require the application of the skills developed in law school.

There are several keys to success in finding a job in a nonlegal career, and these have been stated both explicitly and implicitly throughout this book: Be creative. Look in places where no one else has sought to look. Do not let the naysayers get you down. Think of careers outside the law as more opportunities, and not as second choices. And always remember that your legal training will prove valuable in whatever you choose to do.

Resources

List of Nonlegal Job Titles

The purpose of this list is not to produce a comprehensive list of all the job titles that might possibly be filled with a legally trained individual, but rather to offer a structured inventory of some of the most common job titles for lawyers in nonlegal careers. We encourage readers to view this list as a source of ideas about positions they will be able to pursue, and perhaps think beyond the list to similar positions not included here.

The list is organized in the order that the chapters appear in this book, beginning with Chapter 7 on Corporations. This is a straightforward listing of job titles, and we have not included descriptions of the titles beyond the information that already exists in the corresponding chapters. Readers will note that some titles, such as those involving information technology, appear in different contexts, and are repeated as appropriate. Note also that many of these positions will require additional education and/or credentials, both of which are discussed at greater length in the text.

You may also want to look at the annual employment report *Jobs and JDs,* published by the National Association for Law Placement, available electronically at **www.nalp.org**. The NALP Web site contains other information about careers in business and industry and employment trends that you may also find useful.

porations (Chapter 7)
  Corporate Departments
        Compliance Officer
        Human Resources Manager
        Benefits Manager
        Equal Employment Opportunity (EEO) Officer
        Finance Officer
        Chief Financial Officer
        Budget Officer
        Government Relations and Public Affairs Director
        Consumer Affairs Director
        Public Relations Director
        Transportation Advisor
        Risk Manager
        Regulatory Compliance Manager
        Secretary of the Corporation
        Assistant Secretary of the Corporation
        Purchasing Agent
        Contract Specialist
        Contract Administrator
        Marketing Director
        Security Director
        Security Advisor
        Information Technology Manager
        Intellectual Property Specialist
  Specific Types of Corporations
        Securities Companies and Banks
              Securities Analyst
              Investment Banker
              Commercial Banker
              Financial Analyst
              Stock Broker
        Insurance Companies
              Sales Manager
              Insurance Agent
              Claims Adjuster
              Actuary

Health Care and Pharmaceutical Companies
    Hospital Administrator
    Medical Sales Representative
    Ombudsperson
    Geriatric Care Manager
Real Estate Sales and Development Companies
    Title Agent
    Mortgage Banker
    Mortgage Broker
    Developer
High-Tech Companies
    Programmer
    Systems Analyst
    Contract Specialist
Energy Companies
    Land Manager
    Land Representative
    Environmental Compliance Officer

Government (Chapter 8)
    Executive Branch
        Law Enforcement Agencies
            FBI Special Agent
            Victim Advocate
            Law Enforcement Officer
            Negotiator
        Diplomatic Agencies
            Attaché
            Cultural Affairs Officer
        Intelligence Agencies
            Intelligence Agent
        Regulatory Agencies
            Administrator
            Staff Officer
            Researcher
            Public Affairs Director
            Ombudsperson

Judicial Branch
    Judge
    Judicial Administrator
    Clerk of the Court
    Court Researcher
Legislative Branch
    Legislator
    Legislative Aide
    Legislative Committee Advisor
    Constituent Relations Director
    Media Relations Specialist
The Military
    Military Officer
    Contract Advisor
    Compliance Advisor

Public and Community Service (Chapter 9)
    Professional Associations
        Bar Executive
        Continuing Legal Education (CLE) Administrator
        Association Executive
        Meeting Planner
        Membership Manager
    Political Action Committees (PACs), Lobbying, and Campaigns
        Director
        Lobbyist
        Governmental Affairs Officer
        Researcher
    National and International Service Organizations
        Director
        Executive Director
        Board Member
        Financial Officer
        Public Relations Officer
        Researcher
    Unions
        Union Representative
        Shop Steward

Negotiator
Mediator
Arbitrator
Foundations and Charitable Organizations
Director of Planned Giving
Director of Charitable Contributions
Fundraiser
Fund Manager
Grant Administrator

Professional Services (Chapter 10)
Accounting Firms
Certified Public Accountant
Accountant
Tax Advisor
Analyst
Health Care Firms
Executive Director
Administrator
Manager
Engineering and Architectural Firms
Architect
Engineer
Professional Engineer
Safety Advisor
Environmental Impact Officer
Environmental and Land Use Management Firms
Land Use Manager
Government Affairs Manager
Compliance Officer
Environmental Specialist
Environmental Impact Officer
Counseling Firms
Counselor
Advisor
Crisis Intervention Specialist
Investigation Firms
Investigator

Private Investigator
Personal Financial Services
　Financial Planner
　Stock Broker
　Insurance Sales Representative
Multiprofessional Organizations
　Medical Advisor
　Accountant
　Financial Analyst
　Jury Selection Consultant
　Litigation Support Consultant
　Graphic Evidence Reconstruction Consultant
　Document Manager
　Economist
　Title Abstractor

Publishing and Media (Chapter 11)
　Print
　　Author
　　Writer
　　Editor
　　Publisher
　Radio and Television
　　Producer
　　Assistant Producer
　　Actor
　　News Commentator
　　News Anchor
　　Disk Jockey
　Film
　　Producer
　　Assistant Producer
　　Actor
　　Distributor

Educational Institutions (Chapter 12)
　Primary and Secondary Education
　　Teacher

Principal
Assistant Principal
Dean of Students
Counselor
Parent Liaison
Ombudsperson
School District Administrator
Post-secondary and Graduate Education
Teacher
Dean
Assistant Dean
Dean of Students
Counselor
Pre-law Advisor
Ombudsperson
Career Services Director
Financial Aid Director
Admissions Director
Admissions Recruiting Director
Student Services Director
Academic Support and Counseling Director
Business Affairs Manager
Continuing Legal Education Administrator
External Affairs Director
Fundraising and Development Director
Alumni Affairs Director
Registrar
Human Resources and Benefits Director
Program and Center Director
Information Technology Director
Legal Education
Career Services Director
Financial Aid Director
Admissions Director
Admissions Recruiting Director
Student Services Director
Academic Support and Counseling Director
Business Affairs Manager

Continuing Legal Education Administrator
External Affairs Director
Fundraising and Development Director
Alumni Affairs Director
Registrar
Human Resources and Benefits Director
Program and Center Director
Academic Support Director
Legal Research Director
Information Technology Director
Law Librarian (without faculty appointment)
Lifetime and Continuing Education
CLE Administrator
Lifetime Learning Administrator
Academic Research
Academic Fellow
Research Associate
Academic Researcher

Information and Technology (Chapter 13)
Information Technology Specialists
Technology Consultant
Web Site Designer
Litigation Support Consultant
Document Management Consultant
Graphic Animation Reconstruction Consultant
Document Manager
System Analyst
Programmer
Knowledge Management Specialist

Entrepreneurial Ventures (Chapter 14)
Consultant
Professional Sports Agent
Entertainment Agent
Venture Capitalist
Startup Specialist

Print Resources

The following list of books and publications will serve to start your search. As you will note, most of the entries offer suggestions for further information sources, in addition to the potential employers that are listed. If you have decided on specific areas to pursue, take advantage of these additional references.

Also, there have been many articles published on the subject of alternative legal careers. Search both legal and general media publications for the latest articles and check with your law school career services office or with the law library. The use of LexisNexis or Westlaw will simplify your research by helping you to complete a computerized search of the latest national publications.

Other tools to assist you in identifying resources involve accessing general Internet search engines such as Google or Yahoo. They can lead you to discover many both law-related and nonlegal-career information-resource sites in business, administration, management and other professional fields. Blogs (found by entering "nonlegal or alternative legal career blogs" into the search engine) might provide you with some interesting and often entertaining descriptions of an individual's experiences as a lawyer in a nonlegal environment. Blogs also give you the opportunity to respond to the postings on the site or to ask questions of the owner or other participants. It is always best to search for blogs whenever you have the opportunity. Because of their diary-like nature and their ownership by individuals, new blogs can appear and others disappear daily.

Although the publications are grouped by headings, there is a great deal of crossover. Therefore, feel free to range widely to locate the material that would be most useful to you.

The Legal Profession

Alternative Careers for Lawyers (Princeton Review Publishing, 2000).
This book includes profiles of alternative career attorneys, suggestions concerning how to make the transitions and a resource list that might be helpful for those not yet sure of what they want to do with their training and degree.

America's Greatest Places to Work With a Law Degree, by Kim Alayne Walton, J.D. (Harcourt Brace Legal & Professional Publications, 1999).

This volume includes criteria for evaluation of employment options, describes career opportunities in a variety of settings (including alternative career options), and profiles jobs in both public and private employment. The list of Web sites for various organizations in the resource section of the book is especially helpful to those seeking alternative career opportunities.

Careers in Law, 3rd ed., by Gary A. Munneke, (McGraw-Hill, 2002).

This book provides a comprehensive overview of both legal and nonlegal job opportunities, including substantive practice areas, and practice setting options.

Careers in International Law, 2nd ed., edited by Mark W. Janis and Salli A. Swartz, (American Bar Association, 2001).

This career book is a good introduction to the practice of international law. It includes descriptions of practice related international issues from the perspective of a traditional legal setting to a nontraditional nonlegal organization. The appendix includes many Web sites that are a good resource for those seeking employment with an international focus.

Changing Jobs: A Handbook for Lawyers in the New Millennium, 3rd ed. (American Bar Association, 1999).

A multiauthor book that includes practical advice for lawyers considering a change in careers. Includes all aspects of the job search from the initial decision to change positions through the offer and acceptance process.

Lawyers Career Change Handbook, by Hindi Greenberg (Avon Books, 1998).

This book details the many opportunities available to a lawyer in a wide variety of industries. Each chapter concludes with a list of helpful resources.

JD Preferred! Legal Career Alternatives, (Federal Reports, Inc., 2005).

A book with much information concerning the job search, types of positions available to those with legal training from academic institutions to international business. The resource list could be helpful to those seeking the careers detailed in the book.

Opportunities in Law Careers, by Gary A. Munneke (McGraw-Hill, VGM Career Horizons, 2001).

> Although this book was written with a prelaw audience in mind, it presents an overview of the variety and types of legal opportunities open to law school graduates.

Running from the Law: Why Good Lawyers Are Getting out of the Legal System, by Deborah L. Arron (Ten Speed Press, 2001).

> This book will help you to decide if you still want to enter the legal profession. Describes lawyers who entered traditional law practice and decided it was not the right career choice for them.

What Can You Do With a Law Degree? A Lawyer's Guide to Career Alternatives Inside, Outside & Around the Law, by Deborah Arron (Niche Press, 2003).

> This book is filled with resources, suggestions, and information from lawyers who have made transitions to other professions.

Women at Law: Lessons Learned Along the Pathways to Success, by Phyllis Horn Epstein (American Bar Association, 2004).

> This book provides a wealth of guidance and direction from experienced women lawyers.

Career Planning and Job Search

The Harvard Business School Guide to Careers in Finance (Harvard Business School Press [www.hbsp.harvard.edu], 2002).

> This guide is a detailed review of employment opportunities in finance and investment banking. Company profiles are included as well as a listing of relevant resources both online and in print. The Harvard Business School also publishes the following guide books with content useful to those seeking a career in a corporation or nonprofit institution: *The Harvard Business School Guide to: Careers in Marketing; Management Consulting; Finding Your Next Job;* and *Careers in the Nonprofit Sector.*

Navigating Detours on the Road to Success: A Lawyer's Guide to Career Management, by Kathleen Brady (Inkwater Press, 2005).

> This book provides advice concerning the career planning process from a management perspective. It would be helpful to both students and lawyers in planning their career path.

What Color Is Your Parachute? A Practical Guide for Job-Hunters and Career Changers, by Richard N. Bolles (Ten Speed Press, 2005).

This book does not deal with lawyers specifically; however, it has become a classic in career planning and job search information. The principles it presents are sound and can be used by any student.

The Complete Job Search Handbook: All the Skills You Need to Get Any Job and Have a Good Time Doing It, by Howard Figler (Henry Holt & Co., 1999).

This is another valuable book written for the general reader. It contains valuable information about self-assessment skills and their application to the job search. This book is highly reader friendly.

The Legal Career Guide: From Law Student to Lawyer, by Gary Munneke (American Bar Association, 2002).

This volume provides advice on career planning with a long-term approach to the job search process. It explains the basic legal markets and the transition from the academic world to the professional world of the practice of law.

It's Who You Know: The Magic of Networking in Person and on the Internet, by Cynthia Chin-Lee (Paperback Books, 1998).

A book detailing the most effective and best methods of meeting people for advice and counsel on the job search and career change.

Sweaty Palms: The Neglected Art of Being Interviewed, by H. Anthony Medley (Ten Speed Press, 1992).

An excellent book on interviewing techniques, written by a lawyer, for lawyers.

Vault.Com Career Guide to Consulting, by Doree Shafrir, Maggie Geiger, Hannah Im, and Nici Audhlam-Gardiner (www.Vault.com).

Vault publishes and has available online many resources for both lawyers and business school graduates. The guide on consulting careers includes a description of trends in the profession, a discussion of the life of a consultant, the case interview and the general application process. The resource section has many suggested readings that enhance the information in the guide. Vault also publishes *Vault.Com Guide to Finance Interviews* by D. Bhatawedekhar and the Staff of Vault.Com.

Directories

Guide to American Directories, by Bernard T. Klein (B. Klein Publications).

    Database of directors by title, publisher, and subject category.

Hoover's Handbook of Emerging Companies, 2003 (Hoover's Business Press, 2003).

    Provides information concerning companies identified as being growth businesses. It is useful for its 600 company listings (100 of them in one-page profiles). The profiles provide an overview, list of officers, locations, products or operations, competitors and a chart of financials and number of employees. It would be a good research tool for someone interested in working for a developing business. (This publisher also has a series of business related handbooks available including: *Hoover's Handbook of American Business* (two volumes); *Hoover's Handbook of World Business;* and *Hoover's Handbook of Private Companies.*)

International Information Directory 1998–1999 (Congressional Quarterly, Inc., 2000).

    This directory provides information concerning 4,000 organizations providing international resources within the United States. It is organized by country, subject, and other resources. It would be useful for anyone interested in international policy and its implementation through United States-based operations.

Mergent's Industrial Manual; Mergent's Public Utility Manual; Mergent's Banks and Financial Manual; Mergent's Transportation Manual (Mergent Investor Services—formerly Moody's Investor Services).

Published annually and updated weekly, and written for investors, these manuals provide information about most corporations in the United States, including mailing addresses, organizational setup, holdings, and names of corporate counsel, as well as financial information.

Standard and Poors Directory.
Provides contact information on U.S. corporations.

American Bank Attorneys (Capron Publishing Corporation).
This directory is available semiannually and lists only lawyers who serve as bank counsel. It is organized geographically by state and includes biographical information.

The Foundation Directory (The Foundation Center).
This is an annual roster of foundations together with useful information concerning their work.

AALS Directory of Law Teachers (Association of American Law Schools, 2005–2006).
This annual directory provides a name-by-name listing of teachers and administrators at individual law schools throughout the country.

Encyclopedia of Associations (Gale Research Company).
This encyclopedia is updated annually and consists of multiple volumes: national organizations alphabetically; national organizations geographically; new associations; international associations; and research organizations. The encyclopedia contains much useful information regarding each organization's membership structure, officers and the like. Utilize this resource to determine the best Web and print resources for researching relevant professional associations.

Directory of Trust Institutions (Trusts & Estates).
Published annually, this directory lists the 400 trust institutions in the United States and Canada.

Chronicle of Higher Education. (The Chronicle of Higher Education, Washington, D.C.).
Published weekly, this journal lists teaching and administrative academic positions nationwide. It is also available in an online edition (**www.chronicle.merit.edu**).

Chronicle of Philanthropy.

Published weekly, this journal lists all available positions in organizations and in not-for-profits listing development and marketing positions nationwide. It is available in an online edition.

The Directory of Venture Capital & Private Equity Firms: Domestic & International (Grey House Publishing, 2004).

This directory provides information concerning 3,348 (1,506 domestic and 1,842 international) venture capital and private equity firms (quotes information from the National Venture Capital Association) and provides contact information, location, mission statement, and investment criteria, along with other relevant information.

Additional Resources

The Academic Job Search Handbook, by Mary Morris Heiberger, and Julia Miller Vick (University of Pennsylvania Press, 2001).

This guide book details the opportunities in academic and teaching employment at colleges and universities nationwide. It explains résumés versus vitas, writing samples, research projects, and the application and interview process. The appendix includes a listing of national job listing sites and relevant associations. Although this book is not directed at those with legal training, many lawyers teach at undergraduate institutions focusing on business law, ethics, law and another discipline (health, literature, sciences, etc.).

"The Trail Guide to Environmental Legal Careers," Harvard Law School, Office of Public Interest Advising, Cambridge, Mass. (online at **www.harvard.law.edu/opia**).

Provides information helpful to lawyers seeking to work in a variety of environmental settings including monitoring organizations, and advocacy and policy environmental groups. Includes personal narratives from many lawyers doing environmental work.

Public Service and International Law: A Guide to Professional Opportunities in the United States and Abroad, 4th ed., Harvard Law

School, Office of Public Interest Advising, Cambridge, Mass. (may be ordered online at **www.harvard.law.edu/opia**).

A guide that describes opportunities in inter-government organizations, U.S. government agencies, and nongovernment organizations (NGOs).

Occupational Outlook Handbook, 2004–2005 edition (U.S. Department of Labor, Bureau of Labor Statistics, Washington, D.C.).

This directory is a standard resource for most university and graduate students seeking information concerning future trends in a large number of industries. It is revised every other year and includes information concerning salary expectations, job responsibilities, working conditions, and training opportunities nationwide. It is also available online and can be searched by occupation (see **www.bls.gov** for further information).

Online Resources

American Bar Association Career Counsel (**www.abanet.org**). A virtual career-counseling center that provides advice and resources for those seeking to change careers.

Association for American Law Schools (**www.aals.org**). Provides advice and allows those interested in obtaining a law teaching position to register online for the Law Teaching Job Fair.

American Society of International Law (**www.asil.org**). Provides general information and job listings related to international opportunities in a variety of settings, including policy and administrative positions.

National Association for Law Placement (**www.nalp.org**). Contains information concerning the NALP Foundation's latest research on the profession and has a virtual bookstore with NALP and other organization publications (including federal government employment opportunities, state court judicial clerkships, and many of the books in the ABA career library).

Online Guide to International LL.M. Programs (**www.abanet.org/ legaled**). Annually updated guide gives a comprehensive listing of graduate programs offered by U.S. law schools. It provides details of requirements for admission and concentrations of courses offered.

PSLAWNET (**www.pslawnet.org**). This online publication provides listings of job openings in public interest agencies, fellowships, and teaching positions worldwide. Updated continuously. It is now housed at NALP and can also be reached at **www.NALP .org**.

Council on Foundations (**www.cof.org**). Includes job listings for those interested in obtaining a position with fundraising organizations.

Equal Justice Network (**www.equaljustice.org**). Provides information for lawyers interested in positions in nonprofit organizations and fellowship opportunities.

FindLaw (**www.findlaw.com**). A general site for career information and resources. Provides many links to other organizations and resources. It also contains articles on many topics including career options. The number and scope of available chat rooms can provide helpful information concerning job opportunities in many law-related organizations.

Government Sites: (**www.fedworld.gov**), primary U.S. government site; (**www.fedjobs.com**), job listings for federal agencies; (**www.opm.gov**), U.S. Office of Personnel Management.

Federal Judicial Clerkships (**www.uscourts.gov**). Under employment opportunities, find the link to the Federal Law Clerk Information System, which provides information from judges, listing open clerkship opportunities nationwide. In 2005, more than 400 judges provided their application procedures as an online process. If you are interested in clerking, please check this site often, because procedures change yearly as the online application process is adopted by additional judges. If you are applying as a student, check with your law school career services office as to application dates and requirements. If you are thinking of applying as an experienced lawyer (out of law school one year or more), salaries reflect your level of experience and application deadlines are handled differently from those

The information that you will find helpful is available se sites.

Judicial Clerkships (online information available from mont Law School Web site). Check with your law school to determine whether the career services office has purchased a subscription.

The Riley Guide (**www.rileyguide.com**). This site contains a great deal of helpful information to facilitate the online job search. It has been reviewed favorably by many career experts and it is free to all users. It is easy to use, and the resource lists are unique due to the number of users who send in additional information to be linked. It is often referred to as a "gateway site" for resource information.

Business Job Search and Information Sites: **www.bloomberg.com**, (Bloomberg publications); **www.businessweek.com**, (*Business Week Magazine;* first four issues are free) contains articles concerning business trends and developments; **www .careerbuilder.com**, general career information; **www.dice.com**, jobs in the high tech industry; **www.jobsinthemoney.com**, financial industry positions; **www.fjn.com**, financial and accounting positions; **www.metamoney.com/uslists.index**, contains information concerning the 100 largest U.S. corporations; **www.wetfeet.com**, research corporations also contains directories and job information including the *Insider Guide to Alternative Legal Careers; Beat the Street* (an explanation of banking interviews), *Insider Guide to Jobs in the Computer Hardware/ Software Industry, Insider Guide to Jobs in the Telecommunications Industry,* and *So You Want to be a Management Consultant;* **www.vault.com**, business and law career and job information also publishes many popular occupation specific handbooks and directories; **www.nytimes.com**, *New York Times;* **www .careerjournal.com**, *Wall Street Journal;* **www.fortune.com/ fortune/fortune500**, Fortune 500 site for job listings; Lexis-Nexis, **www.lexisnexis.com/employment/career/**, and WestLaw, **www.westlaw.com/career**, both of which maintain career resource centers with links to articles, directories and job postings including information about alternative legal careers.

General Job Search Sites: **www.hotjobs.com**; **www.careermosaic .com**; **www.lawmatch.com**; **www.employernet.com**; **www .jobfind.com**, job finder; **www.monstertrak.com**; **www.nylj.com**, *National Law Journal;* **www.lawyersweekly.com**, *Lawyers Weekly;* **www.overseasjobs.com**, international job site; **Statejobs .com**, source for state agencies; **www.IdeaList.com**, provides links to nonprofit organizations.

Law School Sites: Many law schools have created special Web-based career resource centers for the use of both students and graduates. The AALS maintains an online list of accredited law schools with links to their individual sites (**www.aals.org**). Check with your law school to find out whether your school's reciprocity policy will allow you access to another law school's online resources.

Higher Education Recruitment Consortium (HERC). In fall 2006, HERC will launch a new Web site that will post, online, open positions at universities within a 50-mile radius of New York City. This is a joint effort of Columbia, NYU, and Yale. Other HERC sites are being planned in New England.

Associations: Most professional associations maintain open Web sites with basic information concerning their mission, membership, and services. These sites often have job postings available (some on the open segment of the site others on a members only password protected segment). Some organizations maintain reduced-cost student membership options. (See **www.d-net.com/columbia** for information on the National Trade & Professional Associations of the United States Directory and the *Encyclopedia of Associations,* Gale Research, published annually.)

Sample Résumé

MICHELLE OFFER
330 Big Apple Street
New York, NY 10023
michelle@michelleoffer.com
(212) 555-1111

EXPERIENCE

INTERNATIONAL CONSULTING COMPANY, New York, NY

Associate   July 2004–Present

Advise commercial banks and other financial institutions regarding organization, technology, and operations. Work with team to analyze, develop and implement recommendations. Maintain high level of client contact with senior executives. Follow-up with clients post implementation.

LARGE INTERNATIONAL LAW FIRM, New York, NY

Associate   September 2002–June 2004
Summer Associate   Summer 2001

In the area of Securities Litigation, defended depositions and prepared outlines in preparation for depositions. Supervised document productions and managed the reviews of opposing parties production. Performed legal research and drafted pleadings, memoranda of law in support of motions to dismiss, and for summary judgment and appeals briefs.

U.S. GOVERNMENT AGENCY, Washington, DC

Summer Intern   Summer 2000

Contacted witnesses, filed motions, compiled trial notes and otherwise assisted in pre-trial preparation, primarily on homicide and repeat offender cases.

U.S. SENATOR'S OFFICE, Washington, DC

Intern   Summer 1999

Assisted legislative aide in charge of business and economic affairs. Replied to constituents' inquiries, researched legislation and helped draft speeches. Compiled press reports from district offices.

EDUCATION

SCHOOL OF LAW, Boston, MA

J.D., *magna cum laude,* received May 2002

Activities: Annual Review of Banking and Financial Law, Staff Member
                   Student Bar Association, Secretary
                   Black Law Student Association, President

UNIVERSITY, Washington, DC

B.A., *cum laude,* received May 1999

Major: Economics
Minor: Political Science
Research Assistant: Department of Economics, Summer 1997 & 1998

INTERESTS: Chess; Competitive marathon running

Index

The Legal Career Guide:
From Law Student to Lawyer,
Fourth Edition

By Gary A. Munneke

This is a step-by-step guide for planning a law career, preparing and executing a job search, and moving into the market. Whether you're considering a solo career, examining government or corporate work, joining a medium or large firm, or focusing on an academic career, this book is filled with practical advice that will help you find your personal niche in the legal profession. This book will also help you make the right choices in building resumes, making informed career decisions, and taking the first step toward career success.

Women-at-Law: Lessons Learned Along the Pathways to Success

By Phyllis Horn Epstein

Discover how women lawyers in a wide variety of practice settings are meeting the challenges of competing in an often all-consuming profession without sacrificing their desire for a multidimensional life. Women-at-Law provides a wealth of practical guidance and direction from experienced women lawyers who share their life stories and advice to inspire and encourage others by offering solutions to the challenges—personal and professional. You'll learn that, with some effort, a motivated woman can redirect her career, her home life, and her interests, in the long journey that is a successful life. If you are a law student, a practicing lawyer, or simply a woman considering a career

The Lawyer's Guide to Balancing Life and Work, Second Edition

By George W. Kaufman

This newly updated and revised Second Edition is written specifically to help lawyers achieve professional and personal satisfaction in their career. Writing with warmth and seasoned wisdom, George Kaufman examines how the profession has changed over the last five year, then offers philosophical approaches, practical examples, and valuable exercises to help lawyers reconcile their goals and expectations with the realities and demands of the legal profession. Interactive exercises are provided throughout the text and on the accompanying CD, to help you discover how to reclaim your life. New lawyers, seasoned veterans, and those who have personal relationships to lawyers will all benefit from this insightful book.

How to Build and Manage a
Personal Injury Practice

By K. William Gibson

Written exclusively for personal injury practitioners, this indispensable resource explores everything from choosing the right office space to measuring results of your marketing campaign. Author Bill Gibson has carefully constructed this "how-to" manual—highlighting all the tactics, technology, and practical tools necessary for a profitable practice, including how to write a sound business plan, develop an accurate financial forecast, maximize your staff while minimizing costs, and more.

How to Build and Manage an
Entertainment Law Practice

By Gary Greenberg

This book addresses a variety of issues critical to establishing a successful entertainment law practice including getting started, preparing a business plan, getting your foot in the door, creating the right image, and marketing your entertainment law practice. The book discusses the basic differences between entertainment law and other types of law practice and provides guidance for avoiding common pitfalls. In addition, an extensive appendix contains sample agreements, forms, letters, and checklists common to entertainment law practitioners. Includes a diskette containing the essential appendix templates, forms and checklists for easy implementation!

How to Build and Manage an Estates Practice

By Daniel B. Evans

Whether you aim to define your "niche" in estates law, or market your estates practice on the Internet, this valuable guide can help you make a practice a success. Chapters are logically organized to lead you through the essential stages of developing your specialty practice and include practical, proven advice for everything from organizing estate planning and trust administration files . . . to conducting estate planning interviews . . . to implementing alternative billing strategies . . . to managing your workload (and staff!). Appendices include such sample documents as: an estate planning fee agreement, an estate administration fee agreement, an estate administration schedule, will execution instructions, and more.

The Successful Lawyer: Powerful Strategies for Transforming Your Practice
By Gerald A. Riskin
Available as a Book, Audio-CD Set, or Combination Package!
Global management consultant and trusted advisor to many of the world's largest law firms, Gerry Riskin goes beyond simple concept or theory and delivers a book packed with practical advice that you can implement right away. By using the principles found in this book, you can live out your dreams, embrace success, and awaken your firm to its full potential. Large law firm or small, managing partners and associates in every area of practice—all can benefit from the information contained in this book. With this book, you can attract what you need and desire into your life, get more satisfaction from your practice and your clients, and do so in a systematic, achievable way.

How to Start and Build a Law Practice, Platinum Fifth Edition
By Jay G Foonberg
This classic ABA bestseller has been used by tens of thousands of lawyers as the comprehensive guide to planning, launching, and growing a successful practice. It's packed with over 600 pages of guidance on identifying the right location, finding clients, setting fees, managing your office, maintaining an ethical and responsible practice, maximizing available resources, upholding your standards, and much more. You'll find the information you need to successfully launch your practice, run it at maximum efficiency, and avoid potential pitfalls along the way. If you're committed to starting—and growing—your own practice, this one book will give you the expert advice you need to make it succeed for years to come.

The Lawyer's Guide to Marketing on the Internet, Second Edition
By Gregory Siskind, Deborah McMurray, and Richard P. Klau
The Internet is a critical component of every law firm marketing strategy—no matter where you are, how large your firm is, or the areas in which you practice. Used effectively, a younger, smaller firm can present an image just as sophisticated and impressive as a larger and more established firm. You can reach potential new clients, in remote areas, at any time, for minimal cost. To help you maximize your Internet marketing capabilities, this book provides you with countless Internet marketing possibilities and shows you how to effectively and efficiently market your law practice on the Internet.

The Lawyer's Guide to Fact Finding on the Internet, Third Edition
By Carole A. Levitt and Mark E. Rosch
Written especially for legal professionals, this revised and expanded edition is a complete, hands-on guide to the best sites, secrets, and shortcuts for conducting efficient research on the Web. Containing over 600 pages of information, with over 100 screen shots of specific Web sites, this resource is filled with practical tips and advice on using specific sites, alerting readers to quirks or hard-to-find information. What's more, user-friendly icons immediately identify free sites, free-with-registration sites, and pay sites. An accompanying CD-ROM includes the links contained in the book, indexed, so you can easily navigate to these cream-of-the-crop Web sites without typing URLs into your browser.

The Lawyer's Guide to Marketing Your Practice, Second Edition
Edited by James A. Durham and Deborah McMurray
This book is packed with practical ideas, innovative strategies, useful checklists, and sample marketing and action plans to help you implement a successful, multi-faceted, and profit-enhancing marketing plan for your firm. Organized into four sections, this illuminating resource covers: Developing Your Approach; Enhancing Your Image; Implementing Marketing Strategies and Maintaining Your Program. Appendix materials include an instructive primer on market research to inform you on research methodologies that support the marketing of legal services. The accompanying CD-ROM contains a wealth of checklists, plans, and other sample reports, questionnaires, and templates—all designed to make implementing your marketing strategy as easy as possible!

The Lawyer's Guide to Creating Persuasive Computer Presentations, Second Edition
By Ann E. Brenden and John D. Goodhue
This book explains the advantages of computer presentation resources, how to use them, what they can do, and the legal issues involved in their use. This revised second edition has been updated to include new chapters on hardware and software that is currently being used for digital displays, and it contains all-new sections that walk the reader through beginning and advanced Microsoft® PowerPoint® skills. Also included is a CD-ROM containing on-screen tutorials illustrating techniques such as animating text, creating zoomed call-out images, insertion and configuration of text and images, and a sample PowerPoint final argument complete with audio, checklists, and help files for using trial presentation software.

30-Day Risk-Free Order Form
Call Today! 1-800-285-2221
Monday–Friday, 7:30 AM – 5:30 PM, Central Time

Qty	Title	LPM Price	Regular Price	Total
_____	The Legal Career Guide: From Law Student to Lawyer, Fourth Edition (5110479)	$ 29.95	$ 34.95	$_____
_____	Women-at-Law: Lessons Learned Along the Pathways to Success (5110509)	39.95	49.95	$_____
_____	The Lawyer's Guide to Balancing Life and Work, Second Edition (5110566)	29.95	39.95	$_____
_____	How to Build and Manage a Personal Injury Practice (5110386)	44.95	54.95	$_____
_____	How to Build and Manage an Estates Practice (5110421)	44.95	54.95	$_____
_____	How to Build and Manage an Entertainment Law Practice (5110453)	54.95	64.95	$_____
_____	How to Start and Build a Law Practice, Platinum Fifth Edition (5110508)	57.95	69.95	$_____
_____	The Lawyer's Guide to Creating Persuasive Computer Presentations, Second Edition (5110530)	79.95	99.95	$_____
_____	The Lawyer's Guide to Fact Finding on the Internet, Third Edition (5110568)	84.95	99.95	$_____
_____	The Lawyer's Guide to Marketing on the Internet, Second Edition (5110484)	69.95	79.95	$_____
_____	The Lawyer's Guide to Marketing Your Practice, Second Edition (5110500)	79.95	89.95	$_____
_____	The Successful Lawyer—Book Only (5110531)	64.95	84.95	$_____
_____	The Successful Lawyer—Audio CDs Only (5110532)	129.95	149.95	$_____
_____	The Successful Lawyer—Audio CDs/Book Combination (5110533)	174.95	209.95	$_____

*Postage and Handling		**Tax	*Postage and Handling	$_____
$10.00 to $24.99	$5.95	DC residents add 5.75%	**Tax	$_____
$25.00 to $49.99	$9.95	IL residents add 9.00%	TOTAL	$_____
$50.00 to $99.99	$12.95			
$100.00 to $349.99	$17.95			
$350 to $499.99	$24.95			

PAYMENT

❑ Check enclosed (to the ABA)

❑ Visa   ❑ MasterCard   ❑ American Express

_____
Account Number   Exp. Date   Signature

Name _____ Firm _____

Address _____

City _____ State ____ Zip ____

Phone Number _____ E-Mail Address _____

Guarantee

If—for any reason—you are not satisfied with your purchase, you may return it within 30 days of receipt for a complete refund of the price of the book(s). No questions asked!

Mail: ABA Publication Orders, P.O. Box 10892, Chicago, Illinois 60610-0892
♦ **Phone: 1-800-285-2221** ♦ **FAX: 312-988-5568**

E-Mail: abasvcctr@abanet.org ♦ **Internet: http://www.lawpractice.org/catalog**